IN THE
SHADOW
OF
HISTORY

TEXAS FOLK-LORE SOCIETY
PUBLICATIONS

NUMBER XV

J. FRANK DOBIE

MODY C. BOATRIGHT   HARRY H. RANSOM

EDITORS

FOLKLORE ASSOCIATES INC.
HATBORO, PENNSYLVANIA
1966

PREFACE TO THE REPRINT EDITION

EVERY folklorist is aware of the interaction between historical events and popular imagination. Whether or not Travis actually drew the line at the Alamo and invited all who would die with him to cross over, this line, says J. Frank Dobie, "is a Grand Canyon cut into the bedrock of human emotions and heroical impulses." It is futile for historians to discount Zuber's account of Rose's story, for "what makes history, whether authenticated or legendary, live is that part of it that appeals to the imagination." And Dobie cared for what is living. He often said that an anecdote of doubtful historicity might reveal more about a man or a people than a bookful of facts.

Dobie had a lifelong interest in the roadrunner or paisano, which he had known since childhood. He made the paisano the emblem of the Texas Folklore Society and also his personal sign. His stationery carried the silhouette of a paisano, and there were carved and painted paisanos of wood and clay in his study. The long article on the paisano that appears in this book has been reprinted in ornithological journals. Dobie divides it into two parts, one for facts and the other for folklore. The popular belief that paisanos surround sleeping rattlesnakes with a corral of thorns increases our interest in the bird, whether or not it is true. It is not merely the facts, says Dobie, but the supposed facts that arouse interest.

To make up IN THE SHADOW OF HISTORY Dobie obtained contributions from several friends and students of his. Tsanoff and Arrowood were teachers at Rice and Texas. Mrs. Kupper, Edward Rohrbough, and Dan Storm studied under

i

PREFACE

Dobie; Mrs. Kupper's thesis on her sheepman uncle was later published by the University of Texas Press. Ruth Dodson was a ranch neighbor of Dobie's in the brush country; her collection of stories about the great Texas *curandero* Don Pedrito Jaramillo, in her translation from her own Spanish original, formed a large part of the Society's volume for 1951. The article by her on the preparation and cooking of tortillas makes a difficult subject perfectly clear.

IN THE SHADOW OF HISTORY contains too many good things to remain out of print any longer.

WILSON M. HUDSON
Secretary-Editor
Texas Folklore Society

Austin, Texas
May 31, 1966

CONTENTS

CONTENTS (*Continued*)

FOLK-LORE AND TRADITION
IN A
GROWING SOCIETY

By RADOSLAV A. TSANOFF

WHAT is the historical and social worth of folk-lore studies? There are some to whom the folklorist is a collector of old wives' tales, an idle fellow, an elaborate and stuffy old gossip. Even when the scope of folk-lore is expanded to comprise popular traditions in general, its critics depreciate its sentimental attachment to a bygone past and condemn it as sterile antiquarianism. The really productive mind, we are told, must cast aside these old crotchets and superstitions and move forward, meet the living problems of today and face the serious future.

This negative estimate of folk-lore expresses a narrow social outlook. Among the factors that have moulded the character of a people are various beliefs and even prejudices, sentiments tragic or humorous, turns of fancy and ingrained convictions, customs, proverbs, songs and arts and handicrafts: the rich and varied treasury of social tradition. This sort of knowledge about a person is essential to a real understanding of his life and character. A true biographer endeavors to enter thus into the inner life of his hero and to recreate it for his readers. Even so, the folk-lore is the sap and savor of a people; you do not know a people, not really, until you have shared in this more intimate life. Those who in one field or in another are exploring the partly buried but still recoverable treasures of popular belief, customs, and tradition in Texas are helping our historians to paint the true

1

colors as well as to draw the outlines of the human landscape in the great Southwest. A lively sense of our traditional heritage is essential to real insight into our past; it ties past and present in a growing society like ours; it assures continuity of social character and institutions and a more intelligent planning for the future.

To be sure, folk-lore is a gossamer tissue of fancy; it falls to pieces under the stern touch of factual research. The folklorist is collecting cobwebs; to get and to convey the full flavor of his tale or custom or quaint superstition, he must himself be half-touched with the delusion and indulge it for the moment. No wonder if he seems uncritical or sentimental, or even "not-quite" to his more sober colleagues. But those quaint fancies and superstitions, and the tales or customs in which they have found expression, reveal the imaginative mood of our people, the tone of their life and thought. Do you say that these folk tales are narratives of that which never actually took place? But what surely did take place was the telling of the tales, themselves the disclosure of a people to him who has eyes to see and ears to hear.

Everyone of us has his moments of day-dreaming when his plans or his fears for himself or others find living expression in his imagination. He may not actually say or do the things he day-dreams about; but if we could enter the life of his imagination, how much better we could understand the life of his actual conduct! Folk-lore is, if you please, the day-dreaming of a people. We can appreciate better the history of people's actual lives if we attend to the stories of their imagination wherein they stand revealed.

This is surely not a plea for sentimental credulity and the inscription of myths in our historical records. The competent historian, in sifting alleged evidence, is bound to unmask a deal of traditional accounts as unreliable in details or even as wholly legendary. But our work is not done when a legend

2

has been unmasked. The legend must also be understood. Why did such a legendary tale gain currency? Though a story has no basis in so-called actual fact, it had basis in the minds in which it found utterance, and those minds are among the facts that we must recognize. Intelligent grasp of any human situation involves the exposure of errors but also requires the understanding and interpretation of them.

The lives of the saints in medieval lore may be no more reliable as detailed record of actual events than the heroic lays of Greek epic or Germanic sagas or than the tales of chivalry that enchanted Don Quixote. But just these differences in partly or wholly imaginative expression show the characteristic features of ancient or of medieval society. Prometheus is affixed to the rock of Caucasus by Zeus; daily the divine bird pecks at his liver and daily it grows again to prolong his torture. The hero refuses to submit himself to Zeus, and waits unyielding for the justice that never comes. But a Christian age sees a different vision: Saint Simeon Stylites standing emaciated on his pillar of stone for more than forty years, waiting daily for the heavenly chariot of the Lord. The three Jewish youths, loyal to the worship of their God, are cast into the fiery furnace of King Nebuchadnezzar, and not one hair on their head is singed by the flames. But Siegfried also rides through a ring of fire, to reach Brunhilde and to rouse her from her divine slumber. So again Siegfried learns the speech of the birds and he hears them reveal the secrets he needs for his heroic adventures. But it is St. Francis who preached to the birds and to the fishes, also, that stood up on their tails in the water and hearkened to his sermon. In each of these stories a certain civilization stands revealed in its visions of hero, martyr, or blessed saint. And if we turn to the tales of chivalry, we are both enchanted and mystified by the fantastic blend of the heroic and the saintly which marked the age of feudalism.

3

Could any of these stories ever have come out of the Rio Grande country or the Panhandle? Our Southwest may have no Argonauts in quest of the Golden Fleece, nor any tragedy of Jason and Medea. But it has its captains of loot and its prospectors of pots of gold, and more pathetic and flea-bitten dreamers, like Dee Davis, town scavenger and "the second sorriest man in Sabinal," of whom our Frank Dobie tells us, working at night and dreaming in the daytime of the golden hoards that would be his, as soon as he can leave his Mexican wife when his boy is twelve years old and the two of them can go prospecting!

Consider the rich Texan heritage of folk-tales, Indian and Mexican legends, cowboy yarns and ballads, stories of treasure-hunter, homesteader, and desperado, pseudo-historical narratives, alleged family chronicles, and pioneer memoirs. How little remains duly attested after the historian's work has been competently done! Frontier life on the open plains is revealed as more humdrum in honest toil and less romantic in crime. The Law West of the Pecos is plucked of its most garish feathers. Much pious ancestral vanity is disillusioned; the sublime heroic note in the memoirs is consigned to the limbo of sentimental indulgence. The cloud of critical reserve is spread over the glowing light of imaginative portrayal, and in place of the richly colored brocade of what might have been, we have before us the sober gray homespun of what actually was.

But surely the real texture of our Southwestern life is neither gray homespun nor rich brocade. It is neither because it is both. We shall never quite grasp and understand our actual living Texan unless we keep in our mind the figures which he keeps before his eyes. Treasure-pirate he often is in his own eyes, and bronco buster, peerless rider of the open plain and carver of empires. This romancing of him is a part of his full history. This is not to say that history is as much

4

truth as fiction, but that history is truer with the fiction in it duly interpreted.

Aristotle said that "poetry is something more philosophic and of graver import than history." What did he mean by this comparative estimate? Surely he did not intend to say that Homer and Sophocles, in their recitals and reenactments of the old Greek myths and popular traditions, were more reliable chroniclers of facts and events than Thucydides or even than Herodotus. This was not Aristotle's idea. What he meant was that the spirit of Greece, the temper and flavor of its life and thought, found supreme expression in the poetic speech of epic and drama. Read Sophocles along with Thucydides and you will get the full story of the Greeks, what they did in detail and also what they essentially were and meant. The historian, Aristotle goes on to say, describes the particular fact, what has been; the poet portrays the universal character, what might be. In truth, there is no opposition here, for the great historian has ever been something of a poet. It is his response to universal meaning in the particular events under his inspection, and his genius to express this meaning, which enable him to see and to make us see with him the living picture of ongoing human life created by a thousand factual dabs of his historical brush.

A lively consciousness and understanding of past traditions, as we have seen, help us to perceive more clearly where we stand; for our present is rooted in the past. It also gives us the right perspective for a more balanced view of our future. I said that the Texan of our day is still in his own eyes a treasure-pirate and a peerless rider of the plains. I mean by this that a certain mental or sentimental temper is apt to survive in social tradition despite radical change in the external conditions of life.

Build our Texas cities on a metropolitan plan, and pile up skyscrapers on the coastal plain or in the Panhandle as high

5

as those of New York; the business and the social life of Texans will still retain their unique regional flavor. And why should we lose this regional flavor, the tang of the Southwest? Our modern life, with its perfect communication of peoples and races, has made each of us a daily spectator of a world-wide pageant, but has smeared us all with a nondescript cosmopolitan varnish, so that we have almost lost our characteristic ways of life and speech and thought. In the folk-lore and traditions of our past we can recognize and cherish and perpetuate things that are distinctively our own. We really cannot afford to lose this precious heritage. We should deliberately seek it out, record and preserve it alive in our imagination and let it color our thought.

Intelligent social planning and legislation must reckon with these intangible but real motive powers in ourselves. The young blood that still thrills to tales of Coronado's Children may not dream of buried chests of gold or of a black sail and skull and crossbones, but it does dream of treasure-hunting and buccaneering just the same. How, otherwise, can we understand the modern epic of the oil-fields, an epic of treasure-trove and prospecting and piracy coastal and inland? The marvel and the magic of the unknown still possesses us, even though our folk-tales move in a different region of ideas. Quack and spellbinder have replaced the magician or the medicine-man of yore, but the lure of the obscure or occult is still with us and confuses our saner outlook on life. Not only the corrupting forces in our complex social organism but also the traditional enchantment of the two-gun hero and desperado plunge hundreds of our lads into lives of crime. And to combat crime and likewise anything else that we may not like, the spirit of the Law West of the Pecos repeatedly finds expression in the framing and in the execution of our legislation. Sound statesmanship, education, public procedure generally, require constant awareness of the social temper

6

with which we are dealing; otherwise, education and legislation alike are apt to prove ineffective or even to defeat their purposes. For only he who is so thoroughly steeped in his past that he is alive and alert to his present, only he can plan intelligently for his future.

Another important thought comes to mind here. The folk-lore of the past expressed the living imagination of a less travelled but also less distracted, less sophisticated but perhaps more reflective age than ours. We have cast most of it away as too old-fashioned for us, but do we have much to put in its place? Ultra-modern as we are, how much of our art and literature, our way of thought and our outlook on life, is a matter of the passing fashion! Little of us has entered into it; it is for us mostly a matter of passive receptivity, surface acquiescence in the fashions of the hour, up-to-date nullity. We live and think on the outer crust of human experience; we do not reach down to the heart, to the root. So we are more learned but less wise than our forebears whose arts and tales and songs we do not often match.

Now folk-lore study is one way of self-deepening. When we get steeped in it, what we do is to enter more fully and intimately into the thought and imagination of those who lived not only on the surface but all the way through. It is only such thorough and genuine living that finds utterance in folk-song. To enter and to share intimately in such lives is a marvelous experience. For as one gets into the very heart of another's life, one's own life is aroused and probed to the heart. It is a mutual experience, like falling in love. A modern mind may thus be discovered and fully revealed to itself. Great artistic achievement is only one example of the power in store for those who have had this communion. So Robert Burns listened to the Scottish folk-songs, and in his soul they sang themselves anew, immortal lyrics. So Richard Wagner fed his imagination on the old Teutonic sagas and turned

7

them into modern masterpieces of musical art. So in the Russian composers the rich treasure of Slavic folk-song was not preserved but re-created. These musicians did not repeat the peasants' songs, but learned from the peasant to feel and to sing in their modern way as he sang in his own way. We get there music that is truly modern yet haunting us with its strain of immemorial beauty.

This is the living power of a society that has not lost communion with its traditions. Poor and ragged, for all its modern trumpery, is a nation that has forgotten its folk-lore and has only its bargain-counter of nondescript fashions and catchwords to take its place! Yet what society is richer in its folk-lore resources than our own? The intimate life of so many civilizations has served to shape our own. Here is treasure all about us. We have to be revealed more fully to ourselves to find new beauty in the old, and wisdom ancient but ever-living. This is the promise of the good and true folk-lorist: reach down, way down into the people's soul; abiding truth and beauty are there.

ROSE AND HIS STORY OF THE ALAMO

I

THE LINE THAT TRAVIS DREW

By J. FRANK DOBIE

IN 1873 the *Texas Almanac* published W. P. Zuber's narrative, "An Escape from the Alamo," to which was appended a statement from his mother verifying the account. It sets forth how a man named Rose appeared at the Zuber home in Grimes County some days after the fall of the Alamo. He was in a pitiable plight physically, starved, his legs full of thorns, his wallet clotted with blood. The Zubers were good Samaritans to him. He told them how in the Alamo on the night of March 3, 1836, Travis had made a remarkable speech to his men; how at the end of it he had drawn a line across the dirt floor with his sword and invited all who would stay, fight, and die to cross over; how all went over, Bowie being carried on his cot, except Rose himself; how he climbed the wall, threw his wallet on the ground, where it soaked up Mexican blood, and how he then got through the cordon of Mexicans and made his way east afoot.

Up to the year 1873, the chronicles of Texas contained no mention of an escape from the Alamo, though the name of Rose had been set down, both in print and in stone, as one of the men who died in the Alamo. Up to this date also, the chronicles of Texas contained no intimation of the speech made by Travis or of the line drawn by his sword. The personal experiences of Rose on his fear-hounded walk across a wide land either uninhabited or now deserted by families who had joined in the Runaway Scrape still makes good reading—a kind of parallel to John C. Duval's *Early Times in Texas*—the story of his escape from Goliad. But this part of the Zuber—or Rose—narrative is minor compared to the speech of Travis, the drawing of the line, and the crossing of the men to his side, four of them bearing the cot on which the shrunken lion Jim Bowie lay.

Here was indeed something new, dramatic and vital to inflame the imagination of the Texas people—a people who, though towers may rise higher than the Tower of Babel to mark the San Jacinto Battlefield and though monuments commemorating events and personalities of history may sprinkle the roadsides from Red River to the Rio Grande, cherish the Alamo as they cherish no other spot either in Texas or in the world beyond. The story seized not only the popular mind; it seized the imagination of story-tellers, poets and historians.

In the very year it was published, Sidney Lanier, a visitor in San Antonio, wrote for the *Southern Magazine*, an essay on "San Antonio de Bexar," which was later included in his *Retrospects and Prospects* and then popularized over Texas by inclusion in William Corner's *San Antonio de Bexar*, 1890, which remains the best history of that city to have been published. Writing on the fall of the Alamo, Lanier comes to Travis's speech and gesture with these words: "On the 3rd of March a single man, Moses Rose, escapes from the fort. His account of that day must entitle it to consecration as one of the most pathetic days of time."

In 1874 or 1875, hard upon the appearance of the Zuber narrative and the refinement that Lanier gave it, Morphis repeated the story in his *History of Texas*. But Thrall's history, which appeared in 1879, gave it only scant mention, along with a slur upon its validity.

The medium that gave the story its widest vogue was Mrs.

Anna J. Hardwicke (Mrs. Percy V.) Pennybacker's *History of Texas for Schools*. No publisher would take the book, and she and her husband issued it themselves, the first edition appearing in 1888. During the next twenty-five years it went into six editions and "several hundred thousand copies were sold, chiefly for use in Texas schools."[1]

To quote from the 1888 edition of this work, which for a quarter of a century gave the school children and also teachers attending the state normals their chief education in Texas history: "On March 4 [*sic*], the Mexicans kept up a terrible cannonade. Just before sunset, this suddenly ceased, and Santa Anna ordered his men to withdraw some distance from the Alamo. The weary Texans who, for ten days and nights, had toiled like giants, sank down to snatch a few moments' rest. Travis seemed to know that this was the lull before the last fury of storm that was to destroy them all; he ordered his men to parade in single file. Then followed one of the grandest scenes history records. In a voice trembling with emotion, Travis told his men that death was inevitable, and showed that he had detained them thus long, hoping for reinforcements.

"When Travis had finished, the silence of the grave reigned over all. Drawing his sword, he drew a line in front of his men and cried: 'Those who wish to die like heroes and patriots come over to me.' There was no hesitation. In a few minutes every soldier, save one, had crossed. Even the wounded dragged themselves across the fatal mark. Colonel Bowie was too ill to leave his couch, but he was not to be deterred by this. 'Lads,' he said, 'I can't get over to you, but won't some of you be kind enough to lift my cot on the other side the line?' In an instant it was done."

In the revised edition of 1895 of the Pennybacker history

---

[1] From an interview with Mrs. Pennybacker published in the Dallas *News*, April 20, 1934.

(and also in the editions of 1898 and 1900) the story of Rose and of the Travis speech was included with extensions, Zuber at the invitation of the author adding many details. Scholars from the first had taken exception to the narrative, generally dismissing rather than discussing it. In Volume 5 (1901-1902) of the *Quarterly* of the Texas State Historical Association Zuber made three contributions in defense of the story; in Volume 6 he made another.

In 1903 Garrison's history appeared—without allusion to Rose or Travis's speech. Doctor George P. Garrison, Professor of History in the University of Texas, became the critic for Mrs. Pennybacker. The very much revised edition of her history that appeared in 1908 omitted, as if it had never appeared, the tale that Zuber ascribed to Rose. In 1913 the Pennybacker history, which had been used so long that some of the men and women who studied it in school saw their own children using it, was supplanted by *A School History of Texas*, by Barker, Potts, and Ramsdell. This kept its place in Texas schools until displaced in 1932 by Clarence A. Wharton's *Lone Star State*, now in use. I wonder if leaving out all reference to Rose and the Travis speech in this book cost Clarence Wharton a twinge.

On page 120 of the first edition of the Barker, Potts and Ramsdell history, under the caption, in black letters, "Some Old Errors," the Rose narrative is bowed out. As Eugene C. Barker has remarked, "Until scientific scholars correct history it is an illusion, and after they write it, it remains an illusion."

The latest study—the most searching that has ever been made—of the battle of the Alamo and the lives of participants, the treatise by Amelia Williams,[2] sums up the matter

---

[2]"A Critical Study of the Siege of the Alamo and of the Personnel of Its Defenders," by Amelia Williams, published in five chapters in the *Southwestern Historical Quarterly*, Vols. 36-37, 1932-1934.

by saying: "Historians have been divided in their opinion concerning this story, the most careful students have discredited it. At best they consider it a legend, plausible perhaps, but almost certainly the creation of a vivid imagination."

But what makes history, whether authenticated or legendary, live is that part of it that appeals to the imagination. Amid many imagination-rousing facts connected with the siege and fall of the Alamo—the superlatively moving letter written by Travis; the picture of Crockett playing his fiddle to cheer the boys up; Bowie on his cot with pistols and Bowie knife; Bonham dashing back from liberty to die with his comrades; the final charge of Santa Anna's men to the strains of the death-announcing *deguello;* the extermination of a hundred and eighty-odd Texans at the hands of an army numbering perhaps five thousand, of whom more than fifteen hundred were killed before the last free man in the walls of the old mission went down; the one sentence entitled to immortality that Texas can claim: "Thermopylae had her message of defeat, the Alamo had none"—amid these and other facts no circumstance has appealed more to popular imagination than the story of how Travis drew the line and invited individuals of the little group to choose between life and immortality. Rose in choosing life got something of the other also, doomed like Carlyle's Doctor Guillotin to wander "a disconsolate ghost on the wrong side of Styx and Lethe."

I was sixteen or seventeen years old when for the first time I went to San Antonio and entered the Alamo, though I had lived all my life not much over a hundred miles away. As I walked through the low door with my father and mother and came into the darkling light of the ancient fortress—ancient for Texas, and a fortress and not a church for Texans—I looked first for the place where Travis drew the line. I never enter the Alamo now but that I think of the line.

13

It is a line that nor all the piety nor wit of research will ever blot out. It is a Grand Canyon cut into the bedrock of human emotions and heroical impulses. It may be expurgated from histories, but it can no more be expunged from popular imagination than the damned spots on Lady Macbeth's hands. Teachers of children dramatize it in school rooms; orators on holidays silver it and gild it; the tellers of historical anecdotes—and there are many of them in Texas —sitting around hotel lobbies speculate on it and say, "Well, we'll believe it whether it's true or not."

Could Rose with his "broken English," no matter how good his memory, have transmitted the Travis speech as we have it from Zuber, who wrote it down thirty-five years after Rose had given it to Zuber's parents, who in turn repeated it to him? Zuber frankly said that he was transmitting only approximation. But it was the kind of speech that the inward-burning Travis might have made, the Travis who wrote "I shall never surrender nor retreat," "I am determined to sustain myself as long as possible and die like a soldier," and whose rubric was "Victory or Death." And for Travis to have drawn the line would have been entirely natural, the more natural because of the fact that in both history and fiction Rubicon lines have repeatedly been drawn for fateful crossings. Because an act has precedent is no reason for denying it. History is sprinkled with momentous sentences spoken by military men at crucial hours. These men about to die in the Alamo must have been conscious of doing a fine and brave thing. Travis certainly thought that he was acting a part that the light of centuries to come would illumine. To have imagination is no reflection on integrity. A magnificent gesture does not abnegate sincerity. Not everything orally transmitted is *mere* legend; there is traditional history as well as traditional folk-lore.

For hundreds of thousands of Texans and others who could

not cite a single authenticated word spoken in the Alamo or a single authenticated act performed by a single man of the besieged group—for these hundreds of thousands of human beings the gesture and the challenge made by William Barrett Travis are a living reality—almost the only personal reality of the Alamo. In a book of reminiscences written by an old cowpuncher of Montana I came only yesterday upon this passage: "The Alamo had fallen. Brave Bob Travis, that drew the dead line with his sword, lay cold in death at the gate."[3] In the "chronicles of wasted time" Travis's dead line belongs as inherently to Texas as William Tell's apple belongs to Switzerland, or as dying Sir Philip Sidney's generosity in refusing a drink of water so that a wounded soldier whose "necessity was greater" might sup it, belongs to England.

For this noble and moving tradition I would register a feeling of gratitude to Louis, or Moses, Rose—a character that from Zuber's narrative and R. B. Blake's study, following this, emerges strangely vivid, even while shrinking and striking back in this, to him, always foreign and bullying world.

Yet it is the thing created and not the creator that the world remembers. Nothing could make a creator happier. Rose has been forgotten, will continue to be forgotten. That line that Travis drew cuts out and off everything else. To illustrate the forgetting and the remembering, too, I will quote from a book dealing with San Antonio, written by an informed newspaper man thirty years ago.

"In the Chapel, sick almost unto death, Bowie lay on a cot, prone and unable to rise. Travis with his sword drew a line across the space in front of where his forces had been assembled. . . . He said: 'All who wish to leave, stand in their places. All who wish to remain and fight to the end cross over this line and come to me.' All but one crossed over to him.

---

[3] *We Pointed Them North*, by E. C. Abbott and Helena Huntington Smith, New York, 1939, 259.

Bowie had his cot lifted and brought over. Rose was the only man who did not cross that line. . . . During the night Crockett lifted Rose up and helped him out of one of the windows. Rose was never heard of after. Probably he perished miserably, butchered before he had gone many yards from the shadow of the structure in which his comrades remained. No one knows his fate, or, if so, it has never been told."[4]

But nobody forgets the line. It is drawn too deep and straight.

Reading the documented historians, you'd think nothing could be so unless it happened. I think Travis made the speech. He certainly made it according to something that the historians might well use—in proper place—to the advantage of truth. In *My Ireland* Lord Dunsany found it necessary to quote a fictional character in order to reveal a historical truth. I want to quote Lord Dunsany himself: "I look, in fact, as much for Ireland in the Irish mind as I do in the Irish fields. Much may pass over a field and leave no trace, but what wonderful tracks we may see where a fancy has passed over the mind."

---

[4]*Combats and Conquests, or Immortal Heroes,* by Charles M. Barnes, San Antonio, 1910, 33-34.

II

AN ESCAPE FROM THE ALAMO

By W. P. ZUBER

[Reprinted from the *Texas Almanac*, 1873, pp. 80-85. The narrative is communicated as a letter, dated from Prairie Plains, Grimes County, Texas, May 7th, 1871.

In the Revised Edition of Mrs. Anna J. Hardwicke Pennybacker's *History of Texas for Schools*, 1895, Zuber retold the Rose story with various added details. In the *Quarterly* of the Texas State Historical Association for July, 1901 (Vol. V, pp. 1-11) Zuber contributed a defense of his narrative, calling attention to the version in Mrs. Pennybacker's "excellent little book."

In the narrative that follows passages enclosed by brackets have been inserted from the narrative in Pennybacker, pp. 183-188.   J. F. D.]

MOSES ROSE, a native of France, was an early immigrant to Texas, and resided in Nacogdoches, where my father, Mr. Abraham Zuber, made his acquaintance in 1827. I believe that he never married. My father regarded and treated him as a friend, and I have often heard him say that he believed Rose to be a man of strict veracity. In 1830, I saw him several times at my father's residence, in what is now San Augustine County. He was then about forty-five years old, and spoke very broken English.

[He had been a soldier in Napoleon's army in the invasion of Russia and the retreat from Moscow. . . . Mr. Frost Thorn, of Nacogdoches, employed him as a messenger between that town and Nachitoches, Louisiana. Said Thorn generally kept four wagons running between the two towns, carrying cotton and other produce to Nachitoches, and returning with goods for Nacogdoches. He arranged with settlers on the road to repair his wagons and supply his teamsters with provender and provisions, on short credit. Rose's duty was to bear the money and to pay the debts thus contracted. At the same time, he carried the mail between the two towns on private contract, there being no government mail on this route. Hence, I infer that he was trustworthy. . . . He was a close observer and had a retentive memory.]

Rose was a warm friend of Colonel James Bowie, and accompanied or followed him to the Alamo in the fall of 1835, and continued with him till within three days of the fall of the fort.

During the last five days and nights of his stay, the enemy bombarded the fort almost incessantly, and several times advanced to the wall, and the men within were so constantly engaged that they ate and slept only at short intervals, while one body of the enemy was retiring to be relieved by another; yet they had not sustained a single loss.

The following is the substance of Rose's account of his escape and the circumstances connected therewith, as he related them to my parents, and they related them to me:

About two hours before sunset, on the third day of March, 1836, the bombardment suddenly ceased, and the enemy withdrew an unusual distance. Taking advantage of that opportunity, Colonel Travis paraded all of his effective men in a single file, and taking his position in front of the center, he stood for some moments apparently speechless from emotion. Then, nerving himself for the occasion, he addressed them substantially as follows:

"My brave companions: Stern necessity compels me to employ the few moments afforded by this probably brief cessation of conflict in making known to you the most interesting, yet the most solemn, melancholy and unwelcome fact that perishing humanity can realize. But how shall I find language to prepare you for its reception? I cannot do so. All that I can say to this purpose is, be prepared for the worst. I must come to the point. Our fate is sealed. Within a very few days—perhaps a very few hours—we must all be in eternity. This is our destiny and we cannot avoid it. This is our certain doom.

"I have deceived you long by the promise of help. But I crave your pardon, hoping that after hearing my explanation you will not only regard my conduct as pardonable, but heartily sympathize with me in my extreme necessity. In deceiving you, I also deceived myself, having been first deceived by others.

"I have continually received the strongest assurances of help from home. Every letter from the Council and every one that I have seen from individuals at home has teemed with assurances that our people were ready, willing and anxious to come to our relief; and that within a very short time we might confidently expect recruits enough to repel any force that would be brought against us. These assurances I received as facts. They inspired me with the greatest confidence that our little band would be made the nucleus of an army of sufficient magnitude to repel our foes and to enforce peace on our own terms. In the honest and simple confidence of my heart, I have transmitted to you these promises of help and my confident hopes of success. But the promised help has not come and our hopes are not to be realized.

"I have evidently confided too much in the promises of our friends. But let us not be in haste to censure them. The enemy has invaded our territory much earlier than we anticipated; and their present approach is a matter of surprise. Our friends were evidently not informed of our perilous condition in time to save us. Doubtless they would have been here by the time they expected any considerable force of the enemy. When they find a Mexican army in their midst, I hope they will show themselves true to their cause.

"My calls on Colonel Fannin remain unanswered and my messengers have not returned. The probabilities are that his whole command has fallen into the hands of the enemy, or been cut to pieces, and that our couriers have been cut off.

"I trust that I have now explained my conduct to your satis-

19

faction and that you do not censure me for my course. I must again refer to the assurances of help from home. They are what deceived me, and they caused me to deceive you. Relying upon those assurances, I determined to remain within these walls until the promised help should arrive, stoutly resisting all assaults from without. Upon the same reliance, I retained you here, regarding the increasing forces of our assailants with contempt till they out-numbered us more than twenty to one, and escape became impossible. For the same reason, I scorned their demand of a surrender at discretion and defied their threat to put every one of us to the sword if the fort should be taken by storm.

"I must now speak of our present situation. Here we are surrounded by an army that could almost eat us for breakfast, from whose arms our lives are for the present protected by these stone walls. We have no hope for help, for no force that we could have reasonably expected could cut its way through the strong ranks of these Mexicans. We dare not surrender; for should we do so, that black flag now waving in our sight, as well as the merciless character of our enemies, admonishes us of what would be our doom. We can not cut our way out through the enemy's ranks; for, in attempting that, we should all be slain in less than ten minutes. Nothing remains, then, but to stay within this fort and fight to the last moment. In this case we must sooner or later all be slain; for I am sure that Santa Anna is determined to storm the fort and take it, even at the greatest cost of the lives of his own men.

"Then we must die! Our speedy dissolution is a fixed and inevitable fact. Our business is not to make a fruitless effort to save our lives, but to choose the manner of our death. But three modes are presented to us. Let us choose that by which we may best serve our country. Shall we surrender and be deliberately shot without taking the life of a single enemy? Shall we try to cut our way out through the Mexican ranks

20

and be butchered before we can kill twenty of our adversaries? I am opposed to either method; for in either case we could but lose our lives without benefiting our friends at home—our fathers and mothers, our brothers and sisters, our wives and little ones. The Mexican army is strong enough to march through the country and exterminate its inhabitants, and our countrymen are not able to oppose them in open field. My choice, then, is to remain in this fort, to resist every assault, and to sell our lives as dearly as possible.

"Then let us band together as brothers and vow to die together. Let us resolve to withstand our adversaries to the last; and at each advance to kill as many of them as possible. And when at last they shall storm our fortress, let us kill them as they come! Kill them as they scale our walls! Kill them as they leap within! Kill them as they raise their weapons and as they use them! Kill them as they kill our companions! And continue to kill them as long as one of us shall remain alive!

"By this policy I trust that we shall so weaken our enemies that our countrymen at home can meet them on fair terms, cut them up, expel them from the country, and thus establish their own independence and secure prosperity and happiness to our families and our country. And be assured our memory will be gratefully cherished by posterity till all history shall be erased and all noble deeds shall be forgotten.

"But I leave every man to his own choice. Should any man prefer to surrender and be tied and shot; or to attempt an escape through the Mexican ranks and be killed before he can run a hundred yards, he is at liberty to do so.

"My choice is to stay in this fort and die for my country, fighting as long as breath shall remain in my body. This I will do, even if you leave me alone. Do as you think best—but no man can die with me without affording me comfort in the moment of death."

Colonel Travis then drew his sword and with its point

21

traced a line upon the ground extending from the right to the left of the file. Then, resuming his position in front of the center, he said, "I now want every man who is determined to stay here and die with me to come across this line. Who will be the first? March!"

The first respondent was Tapley Holland, who leaped the line at a bound, exclaiming, "I am ready to die for my country!" His example was instantly followed by every man in the file, with the exception of Rose. Manifest enthusiasm was universal and tremendous. Every sick man that could walk arose from his bunk and tottered across the line. Colonel Bowie, who could not leave his bed, said, "Boys, I am not able to go to you, but I wish some of you would be so kind as to remove my cot over there." Four men instantly ran to the cot and, each lifting a corner, carried it across the line. Then every sick man that could not walk made the same request and had his bunk removed in like manner.

Rose, too was deeply affected, but differently from his companions. He stood till every man but himself had crossed the line. A consciousness of the real situation overpowered him. He sank upon the ground, covered his face, and yielded to his own reflections. For a time he was unconscious of what was transpiring around him. A bright idea came to his relief: He spoke the Mexican dialect very fluently, and, could he once get safely out of the fort, he might easily pass for a Mexican and effect an escape. Thus encouraged, he suddenly roused as if from sleep. He looked over the area of the fort; every sick man's berth was at its wonted place; every effective soldier was at his post as if waiting orders; he felt as if dreaming.

He directed a searching glance at the cot of Colonel Bowie. There lay his gallant friend. Colonel David Crockett was leaning over the cot, conversing with its occupant in an undertone. After a few seconds Bowie looked at Rose and said:

"You seem not to be willing to die with us, Rose!" "No," said Rose, "I am not prepared to die and shall not do so if I can avoid it." Then Crockett also looked at him and said, "You may as well conclude to die with us, old man, for escape is impossible."

Rose made no reply, but looked up at the top of the wall. "I have often done worse than to climb that wall," thought he. Suiting the action to the thought, he sprang up, seized his wallet of unwashed clothes, and ascended the wall. Standing on its top, he looked down within to take a last view of his dying friends. They were all now in motion, but what they were doing he heeded not. Overpowered by his feelings, he looked away and saw them no more.

Looking down without, he was amazed at the scene of death that met his gaze. From the wall to a considerable distance beyond, the ground was literally covered with slaughtered Mexicans and pools of blood.

He viewed this horrid scene but a moment. He threw down his wallet and leaped after it; he alighted on his feet, but the momentum of the spring threw him sprawling upon his stomach in a puddle of blood. After several seconds he recovered his breath, arose and picked up his wallet; it had fallen open and several garments had rolled out upon the blood. He hurriedly thrust them back, without trying to cleanse them of the coagulated blood which adhered to them. Then, throwing the wallet across his shoulders, he walked rapidly away.

He took the road which led down the river, around the bend to the ford and through the town by the church. He waded the river at the ford and passed through the town. He saw no person in town, but the doors were all closed and San Antonio appeared as a deserted city.

After passing through town, he turned down the river. A stillness as of death prevailed. When he had gone about a quarter of a mile below the town, his ears were saluted by the thunder of the bombardment which was then renewed. That thunder continued to remind him that his friends were true to their cause by a continuous roar with but slight intervals until a little before sunrise on the morning of the sixth, when it ceased and he heard it no more.

At twilight he recrossed the river on a foot-log about three miles below the town. He then directed his course eastwardly towards the Guadalupe River, carefully bearing to the right to avoid the Gonzales road.

On the night of the third he traveled all night, but made but little progress, as his way was interrupted by large tracts of cactus, or prickly pear, which constantly gored him with thorns and forced him out of his course. On the morning of the fourth he was in a wretched plight for traveling, for his legs were full of thorns and very sore. The thorns were very painful and continued to work deeper into the flesh till they produced chronic sores, which are supposed to have terminated his life.

Profiting by experience, he traveled no more at night, but on the two evenings following he made his bed on the soft mesquite grass. On the sixth of March he crossed the Guadalupe by rolling a seasoned log into the water and paddling across with his hands. He afterwards crossed the Colorado in the same manner.

[After ascending a high bluff—the east bank of the Guadalupe—he found himself at a deserted house, at which he found plenty of provisions and cooking vessels. There he took his first nourishment after leaving the Alamo. Travel had caused the thorns to work so deep in the flesh that he could not bear the pain of pulling them out, and he had become lame. There he rested two or three days, hoping that his lameness would subside, but it rather grew worse. Thenceforth he traveled on roads, subsisting, except in the instance to be noted, on provisions which he found in deserted houses. The families were retreating before the threatened advance of the enemy, and between the Guadalupe and Colorado every family on his route had left home. Between the Colorado and the Brazos he found only one family at home. With them he stayed during a considerable time; but probably from want of knowledge or skill, they did nothing to relieve his sore legs.]

He continued his journey toilsomely, tediously and painfully for several weeks, in which time he encountered many hardships and dangers which for want of space cannot be inserted here. He finally arrived at the residence of my father on Lake Creek, in what is now Grimes County.

[The thorns had worked very deep into his flesh, and rendered him so lame that he walked in much pain, and his steps were short and slow. Of course he was feverish and sick. Moreover, he had not changed his apparel since leaving the Alamo. My father supplied him with a clean suit, and my mother had his clothes washed.]

My parents had seen in the *Telegraph and Texas Register* a partial list of those who had fallen at the Alamo, and in it had observed the name of Rose. Having not heard of his escape, they had no doubt that he had died with his companions. On his arrival, my father recognized him instantly, and exclaimed, "My God, Rose! Is this you or is it your ghost?" "This is Rose, and not his ghost," was the reply.

My mother caused her washing servant to open Rose's wallet, in her own presence, and found some of the garments glued together with the blood in which they had fallen when thrown from the Alamo.

My parents also examined his legs, and by the use of forceps extracted an incredible number of cactus thorns, some of them an inch and a half in length, each of which drew out a lump of flesh and was followed by a stream of blood. Salve

25

[which my mother made] was applied to his sores and they soon began to heal.

Rose remained at my father's between two and three weeks, during which time his sores improved rapidly, and he hoped soon to be well. He then left for home. We had reliable information of him but once after his departure. He had arrived at his home in Nacogdoches, but traveling on foot had caused his legs to inflame anew, and his sores had grown so much worse that his friends thought he could not live many months. That was the last we heard of him.

During his stay at my father's Rose related to my parents an account of what transpired in the Alamo before he left it, of his escape, and of what befell him afterwards, and at their request he rehearsed it several times [till my mother could have repeated it as well as he]. Most of the minutiae here recorded were elicited by particular inquiries. In the following June I returned home from the Texas army, and my parents several times rehearsed the whole account to me. At the request of several persons I have here honestly endeavored to make a faithful record of the same.

Before doing so, I refreshed my memory with repeated conversations with my only living parent, Mrs. Mary Ann Zuber, now in her seventy-eighth year, and since the first writing I have read this account to her and corrected it according to her suggestions.

[God had endowed my mother with close observation and extraordinary memory, and I had inherited them. Hence what Rose stated became stamped upon her memory and mine. I admired the sentiments of Travis's speech even as they had come to me third-handed, and not in the speaker's own language. I regretted the apparent impossibility of the speech being preserved for posterity. In 1871 I determined to commit it to paper and try by rearrangement of its disconnected parts to restore its form as a speech. I had enjoyed a slight personal acquaintance with Colonel Travis, had heard repetitions of some of his remarks as a lawyer before the courts, and had read printed copies of some of his despatches from the Alamo. After refreshing my memory by repeated conversations with my mother, I wrote the sentiments of the speech in what I imagined to be Travis's style, but was careful not to change the sense. I devoted several weeks of time to successive rewritings and transpositions of the parts of that speech. This done, I was surprised at the geometrical neatness with which the parts fitted together.]

Of course it is not pretended that Colonel Travis's speech is reported literally, but the ideas are precisely those he advanced, and most of the language is also nearly the same.

Prairie Plains, Grimes County, Texas, May 9, 1871.

I have carefully examined the foregoing letter of my son, William P. Zuber, and feel that I can endorse it with the greatest propriety. The arrival of Moses Rose at our residence, his condition when he came, what transpired during his stay, and the tidings that we afterwards heard of him, are all correctly stated. The part which purports to be Rose's statement of what he saw and heard in the Alamo, of his escape, and of what befell him afterwards is precisely the substance of what Rose stated to my husband and myself.

MARY ANN ZUBER.

III

A VINDICATION OF ROSE AND HIS STORY

By R. B. BLAKE

ONE of the most fascinating sports of the historian is that of tracing a tradition to its origin, and although one may find its origin in the wild romancing of its author, such as Washington's cherry tree myth, there is a certain satisfaction in arriving at the truth, the goal of the true historian, even at the expense of a beautiful drama. But when it is found that folk-lore and tradition meet on a common ground of origin with source material of history, it is an especially gratifying discovery.

Tradition, founded upon facts, is often of more value to the historian than is source material, for tradition is usually the composite view of many people, successive tellers adding a little here and taking away a little there, yet retaining the essence of the story from generation to generation. On the other hand, source material may lead us into gross error in the most essential details; thus the participants in a battle, on opposite sides of the conflict, may write accounts that seem to describe entirely different events, and in order to arrive at the facts, we must get the composite view of many eye-witnesses.

It has been the privilege of the writer to engage in one of these interesting searches among the early records of Nacogdoches County for evidence concerning the story of Moses Rose and his escape from the Alamo during its siege.

For nearly seventy years the account given by Rose of the last speech of Colonel Travis to his companions in the Alamo has been the storm-center of criticism among Texas historians. No corroboration by survivors was possible, and after a time the more conservative historians began to regard the account as a figment of the imagination—some attributing it to the fertile imagination of William P. Zuber, others to the romancing of the old Frenchman, Rose.

But the speech itself so reflects the known characteristics of William Barrett Travis that the story would not down, and so it has lived through all these years in Texas history, though under a cloud of suspicion. When I began to discover corroborations of Rose's story in the official records of Nacogdoches County, and to tell others of what I was finding, I met with the same incredulous smile, but, continuing my search, first among the official records, and then in traditions of the past, I believe I am able at this time to prove that Moses Rose was a man of flesh and blood, that he escaped from the Alamo on March 3, 1836, and that Zuber's account of Rose's story was about as correct as traditional history can ever be.

The old Frenchman's real name was Louis—in the records often spelled Lewis—Rose, Moses being a nickname, though in the records of the Nacogdoches County Board of Land Commissioners the clerk of that body calls him "Stephen Rose," in Rose's testimony concerning M. B. Clark.[1]

For corroboration of Zuber's statement[2] that Louis Rose was a Frenchman, we must rely mainly upon tradition handed down in Nacogdoches, that he was a Frenchman and spoke very broken English.[3] The next statement of Zuber is that he "was an early immigrant to Texas, and resided in Nacogdoches, where my father, Mr. Abraham Zuber, made his acquaintance in 1827." In support of that, I shall first refer to the Certificate of Character issued by John M. Dor, primary judge in Nacogdoches, August 25, 1835, which states that he had been a "resident in this country since the year 1827."[4] Also in appearing before the Nacogdoches County Board of Land Commissioners in the case of Antonio Chirino, Rose testified in February, 1838, that he "knew applicant twelve years, resides here since."[5]

The next statement by Zuber is: "I believe that he never married." Again referring to John M. Dor's Certificate of Character, he says of Rose, "Unmarried, without family."[6] This statement is further confirmed by the power of attorney

---

[1]Proceedings Nacogdoches County Board of Land Commissioners, No. 203, John Forbes, Admr. of M. B. Clark, dec'd.

[2]W. P. Zuber: "An Escape from the Alamo," *Texas Almanac*, 1873.

[3]Account given to R. Lee Brown by Sam Reid as told to author.

[4]University of Texas Transcript of Nacogdoches Archives, Vol. 80, p. 89.

[5]Proceedings Nacogdoches County Board of Land Commissioners, No. 245, James Carter, Ass. of Antonio Chirino.

[6]Nacogdoches Archives, *ibid.*

from Louis Rose to Frost Thorn[7] for "one-third of a league of land to which the said Louis Rose is entitled as a resident citizen [unmarried] of Texas on the day of the date of the Declaration of Independence"; the same statement is made in the deed from Rose to Frost Thorn[8], both being dated June 20, 1837; also by the award of the Land Commissioners,[9] and of the Patent from the Republic of Texas to Frost Thorn, assignee of Lewis Rose.[10]

The next statement of Zuber is to the effect that "My father regarded Rose to be a man of strict veracity." I again refer to Rose's Certificate of Character,[11] in which Dor says, "I, the undersigned, certify that the citizen Louis Rose is a man of very good morality, habits and industry, a lover of the constitution and laws of the country and of the Christian religion." It might be contended that this is simply a form that was followed by the primary judge in all those certificates; but upon the subject of the credibility of Rose as a witness, as bearing upon the probability of the truth of his narrative, I should like to dwell at some length.

The Board of Land Commissioners in Nacogdoches County for 1838 was composed of Dr. James H. Starr as chairman, with Adolphus Sterne and William Hart as associates[12]— three men of the very highest type. Of the first two, nothing further need be said than to name them—they are too well known to the people of Texas; the third member was the second chief justice of Nacogdoches County, a man of the same high type as were Dr. Starr and Adolphus Sterne, men well qualified to pass upon the credibility of the witnesses who appeared before them.

---

[7]Deed Records, Nacogdoches County, Texas, Vol. C, p. 363.
[8]Deed Records, Nacogdoches County, Texas, Vol. C, p. 364.
[9]Proceedings Nacogdoches County Board of Land Commissioners, No. 244, Frost Thorn, Ass. of Lewis Rose.
[10]Deed Records, Nacogdoches County, Texas, Vol. I, p. 107.
[11]Nacogdoches Archives, *ibid.*
[12]Proceedings Nacogdoches County Board of Land Commissioners.

Speaking of the duties of the members of the Board of Land Commissioners, and of his experiences in particular, Dr. Starr in his autobiography says:[13] "The office was of much responsibility, and the duties of extremely difficult performance; especially in Nacogdoches County, which embraced the most populous region of Eastern Texas, including a large number of native Mexicans. Many citizens, especially Mexicans, had already received their headright grants from the former government; but it soon became known to the board that numerous persons of this class were fraudulently presenting claims for certificates. 'Americans' (as citizens of the United States were called) were mainly the criminal instigators of these attempts, bribing the applicants to give false testimony, and agreeing to purchase their certificates when issued. By severe scouting the Nacogdoches Board met with gratifying success in detecting and defeating the attempted frauds; though on more than one occasion threatened with violence by men of mob power (some of them men of prominence) whose applications by the score or more had been rejected."

One of the instances referred to by Dr. Starr was evidently that of General James Smith, who filed in a single lot twenty-four applications, most of which were transfers from Jasper County and elsewhere to Nacogdoches County, supported by written depositions taken before Charles C. Grayson, justice of the peace. The notations made by the board to each of these applications is: "Rejected on ground that the witnesses are unknown to the Board." James Reily, Texas ambassador to Washington, had filed an even greater number of applications, soon after General James Smith filed his, and when this action of the board was made known, Reily refused to present any evidence to the board, and relied upon the dis-

---

[13]*Some Biographical Notes of Dr. James H. Starr, of Texas,* printed for private distribution at Marshall, Texas, 1917.

31

trict court on appeal, and in most of these cases the certificates were granted by the district court. Dr. Starr and his associates always insisted on having witnesses who were known to the members of the board, and upon whose credibility they could intelligently pass.

Louis Rose appeared before the Board of Land Commissioners as a witness for sixteen several applicants for certificates,[14] and in two instances[15] the only corroborating witnesses were Mexican citizens. In other cases[16] the corroborating witness was Adolphus Sterne, a member of the board. In no instance was the testimony of Rose rejected as lacking in credibility.

Continuing our examination into that part of the narrative for which Zuber is responsible, he says: "Rose was a warm friend of Colonel James Bowie, and accompanied or followed him to the Alamo in the fall of 1835 and continued with him till within three days of the fall of the fort." Again examining the records here for data concerning the time of Rose's departure for San Antonio, that date can be very accurately determined from the records. John Durst, on May 8, 1834, deeded to Louis Rose 100 acres of land "in consideration for services rendered," and this land was transferred to Vicente Cordova in Nacogdoches on October 24, 1835.[17]

Referring to the Nacogdoches Archives now on file in Austin, we find a "List of the Effects of the Citizen Louis Rose that by order of the Alcalde Interino Citizen George Pollitt,

---

[14]Proceedings Nacogdoches County Board of Land Commissioners: No. 125, F. H. K. Day; No. 131, Napoleon Dewaltz; No. 203, M. B. Clark; No. 244, Lewis Rose; No. 245, Antonio Chirino; No. 245, James Carter; No. 254, Hrs. of John Blair; No. 268, Admr. Charles Haskell; No. 412, Guadalupe Andrade; No. 428, Hrs. of David Wilson; No. 579, Hrs. of Marcus Sewell; No. 717, Samuel Gilliland; No. 718, James Gilliland; No. 348, 2nd Class, John Gilliland; No. 443, 2nd Class, Stephen Richards; No. 627, 2nd Class, David Musick.

[15]*Ibid.*, No. 269, Charles Haskell; No. 412, Guadalupe Andrade.

[16]*Ibid.*, No. 245, James Carter; No. 579, Marcus Sewell.

[17]Nacogdoches Archives, No. 32 Land Transfers, Office of County Clerk, Nacogdoches, Texas.

the which were delivered to Citizen Vicente Cordova as security for an account and obligation which the aforesaid Cordova holds of the said Rose, which effects were sold at public auction at the exact end of one month, by which they were to cover the obligation and debt that on this date [November 7, 1835] has been presented."[18] This was an auction sale of the household and personal effects of Louis Rose, and was evidently sold after Rose's departure, which was between October 24 and November 7, 1835, and probably immediately after obtaining the necessary funds from Vicente Cordova on October 24.

Before taking up the career of Louis Rose in the Alamo, and afterwards, I should like to make reference to some source material having to do with his occupation and everyday life. One of these is the journal of Frost Thorn's mercantile establishment in Nacogdoches, which covers the period of December, 1833, and January and a part of February, 1834. During this period I have noted seventeen entries against Rose on the books of Frost Thorn, most of them for cash drawn for wages, Rose being a log-cutter and hauler for Frost Thorn's sawmill near Nacogdoches. One item is "To 1 Cast Steel Axe, $4.00." Three charges are for whiskey, one being for one gallon, all three purchases being made within a space of about one week, indicating that he probably drank rather heavily at intervals. On February 7, 1834, Rose is charged with "Sundries for Spanish Woman, $1.00."[19]

Naturally, there is nothing on the records in Nacogdoches concerning Rose's career from the time of his leaving Nacogdoches until the time of his leaving the Alamo. For that reason, I shall next take up the evidence as to the date of his leaving the Alamo, and for this purpose must again refer to

---

[18]University of Texas Transcript of Nacogdoches Archives, Vol. 82, pp. 62-63.
[19]Frost Thorn's Journal for December, 1833, and January and February, 1834. (Original now in possession of J. R. Gray, Nacogdoches, Texas.)

the proceedings of the Nacogdoches County Board of Land Commissioners. Taking these applications in the order in which they appear on the docket of that board, in the case of F. H. K. Day, Lewis Rose testified that he "died with Travis in the Alamo." In the application of John Forbes, administrator of M. B. Clark, Rose "states he saw him a few days before the fall of the Alamo." In the application of the "Heirs of John Blair, decd., by J. Lee, administrator," the testimony of Louis Rose is even more specific, when he states that he "left him in the Alamo 3 March, 1836." Again, in the case of Charles Haskell, Rose testified that he "knew him four years, supposes him killed in the Alamo." In the application of "The Heirs of David Wilson," Rose testified that he "knew him before the 2nd May 1835, was in the Alamo when taken." And finally, in the application of "The Heirs of Marcus Sewell," Louis Rose stated that he "knew him in the Alamo and left him there three days before it fell."[20]

Rose was probably born in France about 1785. He was an enuthusiastic follower of the "Little Corporal" in his triumphant invasion of Russia; he endured the hardships of the disastrous retreat from Moscow, through the snow and intense cold of the Russian winter of 1812; and he doubtless followed the vicissitudes of Napoleon Bonaparte's career to its disastrous termination on the field of Waterloo. My surmise then is that Rose attached himself to the band of refugees under the command of General Lallemand, seeking a home in the New World. Instead of proceeding with Lallemand to the settlement on the Trinity River, Rose probably came to Louisiana, remaining there until Haden Edwards

---

[20]Proceedings Nacogdoches County Board of Land Commissioners: No. 125, F. H. K. Day by Moses L. Patton and the Heirs of Henry Teal, assignees; No. 203, John Forbes, Admr. of M. B. Clark, decd.; No. 254, The Heirs of John Blair, decd., by J. Lee, Admr.; No. 269, George Pollitt, Admr. of Charles Haskell; No. 427, The Heirs of David Wilson by George Pollitt, Admr.; No. 579, The Heirs of Marcus Sewell by John McDonald, Admr.

recruited men in November, 1826, for the Fredonian Rebellion, when he came to Nacogdoches—1826 being the date he came to Nacogdoches according to his own testimony.[21]

After the Fredonian fiasco, Rose remained in the neighborhood of Nacogdoches, probably living the greater part of the time among the Mexican population until the Battle of Nacogdoches, on August 2, 1832, when Adolphus Sterne and James Carter became acquainted with him.[22] Especial significance is attached to their statement that they became acquainted with Rose in 1832, because the little band of seventeen Texans who captured the entire Mexican garrison on August 3, 1832, was led by James Carter and piloted by Adolphus Sterne.

Following the Battle of Nacogdoches, and his alignment with the American element there, Louis Rose became a more definite fixture in Nacogdoches County, or department as it was then known. John Durst employed him in the operation of his sawmill near the site of the Old Presidio, east of the Angelina River[23]; and Frost Thorn at his sawmill south of Nacogdoches.[24]

Soon after the departure of Thomas J. Rusk's company for the siege of Béxar, about the middle of September, 1835, the old roving "soldier of fortune" spirit was again aroused in Rose. October 7, 1835, he borrowed what money he could from Vicente Cordova, who was later to head the Cordova Rebellion, pledging his household goods and personal belongings as security for the loan. Needing still more cash, he sold his Walke ranch west of the Angelina River to the same party. Having purchased necessary supplies—horse, blankets,

---

[21]Proceedings Nacogdoches County Board of Land Commissioners, No. 245, James Carter, Ass. of Antonio Chirino.

[22]Proceedings Nacogdoches County Board of Land Commissioners, No. 244, Frost Thorn, Ass. of Lewis Rose.

[23]Nacogdoches Archives, Land Transfers No. 32, Office of County Clerk of Nacogdoches County, Texas.

[24]Frost Thorn's Journal for December, 1833, and January and February, 1834. (Original now in possession of J. R. Gray, Nacogdoches, Texas.)

etc.—he left Nacogdoches about the end of October, 1835, headed for Béxar, probably in company with other volunteers from Nacogdoches, possibly in the company commanded by William H. Landrum.

During the tedium of the siege of Béxar, many of the volunteers from Nacogdoches returned to their homes, dissatisfied with the inaction; but Rose and many others remained until the capture of the city, when he and more than a score of other Nacogdoches volunteers were left with the garrison there, afterwards retiring to the Alamo upon the approach of Santa Anna's army, where he remained until March 3, 1836.

We will now take up Zuber's narrative for the remainder of his stay in the Alamo and subsequent escape. Zuber says: "During the last five days and nights of his stay, the enemy bombarded the fort almost incessantly, and several times advanced to the wall, and the men within were so constantly engaged that they ate and slept only at short intervals, while one body of the enemy was retiring, to be relieved by another, yet they had not sustained a single loss.[25]

After giving the speech made by Travis, which he does not pretend to be verbatim, Zuber says: "Rose remained at my father's between two and three weeks, during which time his sores improved rapidly and he hoped soon to be well. He then left for home."

Taking up the evidence in Nacogdoches again at that point, the first we see of him back at home is an account on the general ledger of Logan & Raguet's mercantile establishment, page 58, under dated of May 10, 1836, amounting to $20.75.[26]

The next record showing Louis Rose's presence in Nacog-

---

[25]See also Letter from W. Barrett Travis to the Convention, dated March 3, 1836. Southwestern Historical *Quarterly*, Vol. XXXVII, pp. 23-24, Miss Amelia Williams, "A Critical Study of the Siege of the Alamo."

[26]Probate Records, Nacogdoches County, Estate of Wm. G. Logan. Inventory of the Estate.

doches is that of the power of attorney and deed executed by Rose to Frost Thorn for his one-third league certificate, already referred to, which was executed in Nacogdoches on June 20, 1837.

Turning to the criminal records of Nacogdoches County, we find the next reference to Louis Rose as a witness in the case of The Republic of Texas vs. Milton Shropshire, charged with the murder of Amos Donavan on July 17, 1837. The proceedings of the examining trial show his presence in Nacogdoches both on the night of the homicide, July 17, 1837, and on the day of the examining trial, July 26, 1837. The record here seems to disclose another nickname Rose had acquired following his escape from the Alamo, the County Clerk, Daniel Lacey, referring to him as Luesa Rose, using the feminine form of Louis, probably a stab at his lack of courage.[27]

Following this are his sixteen appearances as a witness before the Nacogdoches County Board of Land Commissioners, already referred to, during the spring of 1838. Then again turning to the records of the criminal court of Nacogdoches County, we find the account of an examining trial of one Francisco Garcia for an assault to murder committed upon Louis Rose, April 10, 1838, the evidence[28] in the case showing that the Mexican was crazy drunk at the time of the assault, and probably did not know what he was doing. Rose's testimony, as recorded is: "I was starting about my own business. A man at Thorn's yard called after me; supposed he was groggy and did not answer; the man was the prisoner. Prisoner ran after me, came near the graveyard, presented a pistol. I threw down my axe, took hold of the pistol to prevent

[27]Examining Trial Papers, Republic vs. Milton Shropshire, in Archives of Stephen F. Austin State Teachers College, Nacogdoches, Texas.
[28]Cause No. 65—Republic of Texas vs. Francisco Garcia. Examining Trial Papers, in Archives of Stephen F. Austin State Teachers College, Nacogdoches, Texas.

his shooting me. Prisoner let go of the pistol and took up my knife, which I had thrown down. When he took the knife he rushed upon me with the knife. I then snapped pistol at him. He went to cutting me with the knife and I shot the pistol at him. He wounded me in the back. After I shot him, he caught hold of me and threw me down. I escaped from him and ran. I wounded him with the knife. When he came to me he said, 'Stop! I want to kill you'."

There is also the record of the court in this case, showing the indictment, continuance and final quashing of the indictment because it was faulty in form.[29]

On December 5 and 17, 1839, and again on January 3, 1840, records of Rose as a witness before the Nacogdoches County Board of Land Commissioners indicate that he probably at that time lived in what is now Cherokee County.[30]

The last record evidence concerning Louis Rose is from the account of James H. Starr, administrator of the estate of Kelsey H. Douglass, filed August 1, 1842, showing Louis Rose's note, received June 14, 1842, for $7.75, with $1.09 as the amount of interest paid on the account for which the note was given.[31]

This completes the record evidence to be considered in our sketch of Louis Rose. The traditional evidence, concerning the last eight or ten years of Rose's life, was obtained in the main from State Representative R. Lee Brown, of Nacogdoches, Texas, who had heard some of the anecdotes related by Mr. Sam Reid, son of one of the early settlers of Nacogdoches, as well as the account of Rose's last days as related to Mr. Brown by his step-grandmother, a daughter of Aaron

---

[29]Complete Records District Court of Nacogdoches County, Vol. A, p. 253.

[30]Proceedings Nacogdoches County Board of Land Commissioners. No. 348, 2nd Class, John Gilliland; No. 443, 2nd Class, Stephen Richards; No. 627, David Musick; No. 717, Samuel Gilliland; No. 718, James Gilliland.

[31]Probate Court of Nacogdoches County, Texas, Record of Accounts of Executors and Administrators, Book A, pp. 24-25.

Ferguson, with whom Louis Rose lived during the last years of his life.

Soon after the Texas Revolution, Louis Rose operated a meat market, located about half a block east of the Old Stone Fort, facing a narrow alley, now known as Commerce Street. Across the alley was the old Mexican bull pen, where bull fights were held in the early days, enclosed with a high board fence.

Two anecdotes of the meat market days, as related by Mr. Sam Reid, throw light on Rose's temperament. One day John R. Clute, who had come to Nacogdoches from New York prior to the revolution and was a well known character here during years that followed, dropped into Rose's market to complain of some unusually tough beef he had gotten there. Rose became enraged at Clute's complaint and turned around to get a loaded shotgun hanging on the wall. But his customer, seeing what Rose was reaching for, leaped for the street, vaulted the high fence around the bull pen and disappeared before Rose could fire. Moses turned, placed the gun back on the rack and said, "Oh, well, he has gone. I will let him go."

On another occasion when a customer was complaining of the toughness of his beef, he grabbed the man, seized a Bowie knife, sharp as a razor, lying on his cutting block, and drew it across the customer's stomach, cutting entirely through his clothing, though barely drawing blood from his body. Rose told him, with an oath, "If you come in here complaining again, I'll cut you half in two."

Mr. Reid used to tell that he had on several occasions heard acquaintances of Rose ask him: "Mose, why didn't you stay there in the Alamo with the others?" The invariable reply was: "By God, I wasn't ready to die."

Rose is described by those who knew him as being illiterate, and he always signed his name with his mark. Tradition says that he was of a restless, roving disposition, never re-

39

maining in one employment for very long at a time. During the early forties he is said to have left Nacogdoches, first going to Nachitoches, Louisiana, and finally drifting to the home of Aaron Ferguson, six and one-half miles northeast of Logansport, Louisiana.

Aaron Ferguson's daughter—who married a man by the name of Walker—remembered Rose, seeing him many times on her visits to her father's home after her marriage and removal to Harrison County, Texas. This daughter said that the old man was a great deal of trouble during the later years of his life, as a result of the chronic sores caused by the cactus thorns in his legs, picked up during his flight from the Alamo, as described by William P. Zuber at a later date; she also said that for some time prior to his death, at the age of sixty-odd years, Rose was bed-ridden by reason of those chronic sores.

A short time ago I stood in the old abandoned Ferguson cemetery, overgrown with trees, with scores of graves marked only by a slight depression in the earth, and pondered which depression might mark the last resting place of the soldier of fortune.

East of the cemetery, about two hundred and fifty yards, is the site of the old Aaron Ferguson home, on which now stands a small house, built of logs and covered over during the last few years with boards, thought by some to be the original home of Aaron Ferguson, where Louis Rose passed his last days, probably dreaming of the days when he followed the conquering Napoleon, forgotten by the world, with not even a bounty or donation warrant from the Republic of Texas for his services.

Doubtless the most enduring monument to the memory of Louis Rose is his account of the last great speech of Colonel William Barret Travis to his comrades in the Alamo, and may we hope that in the future that monument, at least, will be accorded to him. Probably Rose was peculiarly fitted to carry this speech to the people of Texas, because of the fact that he could not read and write, and had, for that reason, trained his memory to retain what he heard.

INVENTING STORIES ABOUT THE ALAMO

W. P. ZUBER to CHARLIE JEFFRIES

FROM my earliest years I read everything I came across in any way pertaining to the Alamo; the appetite has never slackened. As a youth I would occasionally come across something, maybe a work of fiction, maybe something that purported to be straight history, painfully at variance with what Anna J. Pennybacker had taught us. So one day I decided to write William P. Zuber, about the last representative of the Texans who had fought in the Revolution and a man whom I considered as being intelligent with first-hand information. I asked him about Rose's escape from the Alamo, his estimate of the casualties on both sides during the battle, and whether he knew any surviving Mexicans. If he did know any survivors, my notion was to hunt them up and get whatever they had to say. The letter that follows came in reply to my inquiries.

Iola, Texas, August 17th, 1904.

Mr. C. C. Jeffries,
Winkler, Texas.
My Dear Sir:

Your letter of the 4th instant has been to hand during several days, but recent absence and ill health have delayed my reply till now.

My conviction is that every one of our 181 men in the Alamo fought till slain, unless we except Colonel James Bowie, who being prostrate with pneumonia, and not able to rise, was murdered in his cot after the rest were all killed, and who it was said that, from his cot, he fired two effective shots from his pistols at his murderers. I do not believe that any one of them surrendered or asked for quarters, for they all knew that the Mexicans would not spare the life of a man. It is not probable that any one of the Mexicans who stormed the fort now lives.

The storming of the Alamo was brisk work. The assault was made at dawn, and by a little after sunrise every defender was slain.

I happen to know how some of the absurd stories of alleged Alamo incidents originated. On the night of March 13, 1836, Captain Joseph L. Bennett's company, including myself, being en route for the Alamo, camped on the edge of the Colorado bottom, east of the river, where the town of La Grange now is. Just at dusk of evening, Colonel J. C. Neill rode into our camp and informed us of the disaster. His statement was that on the 8th of March he was en route from Gonzales to the Alamo. I did not understand his purpose, but I now judge that it may have been to resume command of the garrison. On that day (March 8) at the Cibola he met Mrs. Dickinson, who was in the fort when it fell; but being a noncombatant, and shut up in a room, was not killed. There she told him of the lamentable event, and he returned toward the east. He seems to have passed Gonzales without halting to inform General Houston, our little force at that place, nor the people of the town of the great calamity. I know not why, for while he was stating the facts to us—*at that precise moment*—Mrs. Dickinson was stating the same to General Houston at Gonzales, 45 miles nearer than our camp to the Alamo. He did not dismount at our camp, but, after delivering the sad news to us, he rode away.

Just as Colonel Neill rode into our camp, four young men arrived from the settlement around Bastrop. They had assisted their families to start on "the run-away scrape," and were proceeding down the Colorado to join a company of volunteers for the army—so they said. They camped at my mess-fire, opposite the side occupied by us. We all sat up late talking of the sad news brought by Colonel Neill, and one of the four young men entertained us with recitals of many alleged incidents of the fall of the Alamo. I was a lad, and believed all that he said; of course inferring that he had seen Mrs. Dickinson, and learned the facts from her.

On the next morning, soon after early breakfast, they left us, but, before their departure, I asked one of the gassy man's comrades where they had seen Mrs. Dickinson. He replied that they had not seen her at all.

"Then," said I, "how did you learn so much about the fall of the Alamo?"

"We never heard of it," said he, "till our arrival here last night, and know no more about it than you know."

"Why," said I, "one of your comrades told us last night of many incidents of that event. How did he learn them?"

"Oh!" said he, "you ought not to listen to him. He talks to hear himself talk; and spins yarns as fast as he can talk."

I was astonished. I had been badly gulled and was ashamed of my credulity. But some members of our company treasured the gasser's scraps of intelligence, and after we joined the main army repeated them to others, who repeated them again, and thus they were broadly distributed. After the battle of San Jacinto, some of our men repeated them interrogatively to prisoners, inquiring if they were true, and many of them, to seem intelligent, confirmed them, answering in effect, "Yes, that is true. I saw it." These yarns spread from mouth to ear, as facts, among the prisoners, and even some of their generals utilized them in modified form in efforts to prove themselves innocent of the outrages perpetrated by their countrymen. I refer especially to the yarns of one idle talker, because I witnessed them, but doubtless others did likewise, with similar results.

44

I recite one of the gasser's yarns as a sample of the whole, and give it, as I remember it, nearly in his own words. He said substantially: "The Texans all fought bravely, till all but six were killed. Then the six called for quarters, but were answered, 'No quartero.' Then the six fought till all but one were killed. Then the one cried for quarters, surrendered, and was conducted to Santa Anna, who ordered his soldiers to execute him. Then six Mexicans formed a circle around him, each drove his bayonet into him, and the six lifted him, on their bayonets, above their heads." I repeat the substance of this yarn, because, after being repeated with several variations, it found its way, in one form, into Mexican history, and thence into a footnote into Bancroft's *History of Texas*.

Another version of this story—referring to the six men— is that, after the battle, some washerwomen discovered six men hiding under a bridge and reported them; they were conducted to Santa Anna, and an officer begged him to spare their lives, but he caused them to be executed immediately.

The Mexican general, Cos, while a prisoner, referring to the one man, applied the story to himself—doubtless in hope thereby to mitigate his condition as a captive. He stated it to the late Dr. George M. Patrick, late of Anderson, Texas. I state his recital as Dr. Patrick stated it to me. When the Mexican prisoners were quartered at Anahuac, in 1836, Dr. Patrick visited them and obtained an interview, through an interpreter, with General Cos. He asked Cos if he saw Colonel David Crockett in the Alamo, and if he knew how he died.

Cos replied: "Yes, sir. When we thought that all the defenders were slain, I was searching the barracks, and found, alive and unhurt, a fine-looking and well-dressed man, locked up, alone, in one of the rooms, and asked him who he was. He replied: 'I am David Crocket, a citizen of the State of Tennessee and representative of a district of that State in the United States Congress. I have come to Texas on a visit of exploration; purposing, if permitted, to become a loyal citizen of the Republic of Mexico. I extended my visit to San Antonio, and called in the Alamo to become acquainted with the officers, and learn of them what I could of the condition of affairs. Soon after my arrival, the fort was invested by government troops, whereby I have been prevented from leaving it. And here I am yet, a noncombatant and foreigner, having taken no part in the fighting.'

"I proposed [Cos is narrating] to introduce him to the President, state his situation to him, and request him to depart in peace, to which he thankfully assented. I then conducted him to the President, to whom I introduced him in about these words: 'Mr. President, I beg permission to present to your Excellency the Honorable David Crockett, a citizen of the State of Tennessee and Representative of a district of that State in the United States Congress. He has come to Texas on a visit of exploration; purposing, if permitted, to become a loyal citizen of the Repbulic of Mexico. He extended his visit to San Antonio, and called in the Alamo to become acquainted with its officers and to learn of them what he could of the condition of affairs. Soon after his arrival, the fort was invested by Government troops, whereby he has been prevented from leaving it. And here he is yet, noncombatant and foreigner, having taken no part in the fighting. And now, Mr. President, I beseech your Excellency to permit him to depart in peace.'

"Santa Anna heard me through, but impatiently. Then he replied sharply, 'You know your orders'; turned his back upon us and walked away. But, as he turned, Crockett drew from his bosom a dagger, with which he smote at him with a thrust, which, if not arrested, would surely have killed him; but was met by a bayonet-thrust by the hand of a soldier through the heart; he fell and soon expired." This story by

Cos, though a gross falsehood, shows what Santa Anna would have done if it were true.

Exposure of the origin of some of the myths related of the fall of the Alamo shows how easily the lies of idle talkers may find their way into history; but the truth alone is vastly wonderful. Some of our historians seem reluctant to tell the whole truth from fear of being discredited. My estimates are that the defenders of the Alamo numbered 181 men; that their assailants outnumbered them more than twenty to one, and that the loss of the latter during the siege of thirteen days, including the final assault, was nearly or quite one thousand men. All reliable reports of the battle concur in the idea that not one Texan of the 181 escaped or surrendered, or tried to do so; but every man of them died fighting.

Yours truly,

W. P. ZUBER.

HOW JIM BOWIE DIED

By EDWARD G. ROHRBOUGH

JAMES BOWIE was a man of great physical strength and endurance. He possessed unusual resourcefulness, and he was equal to extraordinary emergencies; yet when the most important crisis of his life came, it found him sick and helpless, on the flat of his back. There is nothing colorful or romantic about illness. The very fact that Bowie was desperately ill, however, made his death superlatively courageous in the eyes of men, and the manner of his death, as variously narrated, became a symbol of Texan courage. If the defenders of Texas fought from their very death beds, how could they be defeated?

The stories of Bowie's death are as different in details as the stories of the origin of the Bowie knife or the stories of the lost mine to which Bowie gave his name. One of the most stirring stories of Bowie's death was told by W. P. Zuber, who claimed to have heard it from a Mexican—one of Santa Anna's fifers, named Apolinario Saldigna. This name was shortened to Polin by the man's friends. At the time of the battle, Polin was sixteen years old. Zuber retold Polin's story in the following manner:

> After the fort (the celebrated church of the Alamo at San Antonio) had been stormed and all of its defenders had been reported to have been slain, and when the Mexican assailants had been recalled from within the walls, Santa Anna and his staff entered the fortress. Polin, being a fifer, and therefore a privileged person, and possibly more so because of his tender years, by permission, entered with them. He desired to see all that was to be seen, and for this purpose he kept himself near his general

48

in chief. Santa Anna had ordered that no corpses should be disturbed till after he had looked upon them all, and seen how every man had fallen. He had employed three or four citizens of San Antonio to enter with him, and to point out the bodies of several distinguished Texans.

The principal corpses that Santa Anna desired to see were those of Colonel W. Barrett Travis, Colonel James Bowie, and another man whose name Polin could not remember, but which, by his description, must have been Crockett.

On entering the fort, the eyes of the conqueror were greeted by a scene which Polin could not very well describe. The bodies of the Texans lay as they had fallen, and many of them were covered by the bodies of the Mexicans who had fallen upon them. The close of the struggle seemed to have been a hand-to-hand engagement, and the number of dead Mexicans exceeded that of Texans. The ground was covered by the bodies of the slain. Santa Anna and his suite for a long time wandered from one apartment of the fortress to another, stepping over and on the dead, seemingly enjoying this scene of human butchery.

After a general reconnoitering of the premises, the Dictator came upon the body of Colonel Travis. After viewing the form and features a few moments, Santa Anna thrust his sword through the dead man's body and turned away. He was then conducted to the remains of the man (Crockett) whose name Polin could not remember. This man lay with his face upward, and his body was covered by those of many Mexicans who had fallen upon him. His face was florid like that of a living person, and he looked like a healthy man asleep. Santa Anna viewed him for a few moments, thrust his sword through his breast and turned away.

The one who had come to point out certain bodies made a long but unsuccessful search for that of Colonel Bowie, and reported to Santa Anna that it was not to be found.

Then a detail of Mexican soldiers came into the fort. They were commanded by two officers, a captain and a junior officer whose title Polin could not explain, but whom I shall, for convenience, call Lieutenant. They were both quite young men, very fair, very handsome, and so nearly alike in complexion, form, size, and features, that Polin judged them to be brothers, the captain being apparently a little older than the other. Polin did not remember to have seen them before, was confident that he never saw them afterward, and he did not learn their names.

After the entry of the detail, Santa Anna and his suite retired, but the two officers and their men remained within. The two kept themselves close together, side by side. Polin was desirous to know what was to be done, and remained with the detail and to enable himself to see all that was to be seen, he kept near the two officers, never losing sight of them.

As soon as the Dictator and his suite had retired, the squad began to take up the dead Texans, and to bring them together, and to lay them in a pile, but before thus depositing them, the Mexicans rifled the pockets, and in many cases stripped the bodies of all clothing.

The two officers took a stand about the center of the arena. The first corpse was brought and laid as the captain directed. This formed a nucleus for a pile. The bodies were brought successively each by four men, and dropped near the captain's feet. In imitation of his general, the captain viewed the body of each dead Texan for a few moments, and thrust his sword through it, after which the mutilated corpse was cast upon the heap at another motion of the captain's sword.

When all the Texans had been thrown on the pile, four soldiers walked around it, each carrying a pan of camphene, that was poured upon the bodies for a funeral pyre. This process was continued until all the bodies were thoroughly wetted. . . .

While the fluid was being thrown upon the pile, four soldiers brought a cot, on which lay a sick man, and set it down by the captain and one of them remarked, "Here, captain, is a man that is not dead." "Why is he not dead?" asked the captain. "We found him in a room by himself," said the soldier. "He seems to be very sick, and I suppose he was not able to fight, and was placed there by his companions, to be in a safe place and out of the way." The captain gave the sick man a searching look

50

and said, "I think I have seen this man before." The lieutenant replied, "I think I have, too," and, stooping down, he examined his features closely. Then raising himself, he addressed the captain, "He is no other than the infamous Colonel Bowie."

The captain then also stopped, gazed intently upon the sick man's face, assumed an erect position, and confirmed the conviction of the lieutenant.

The captain looked fiercely upon the sick man and said: "How is it, Bowie, you have been found hidden in a room by yourself and have not died fighting, like your companions?" To which Bowie replied in good Castilian: "I should certainly have done so, but you see I am sick and cannot get off this cot." "Ah, Bowie," said the captain, "you have come to a *fearful* end—and well do you deserve it. As an immigrant to Mexico you have taken an oath before God to support the Mexican Government; but you are now violating that oath by fighting against that government which you have sworn to defend. But this perjury, common to all your rebellious countrymen, is not your only offense. You have married a respectable Mexican lady and are fighting against her countrymen. Thus you have not only perjured yourself, but you have also betrayed your own family."

"I did," said Bowie, "take an oath to support the Constitution of Mexico, and in defense of that Constitution I am now fighting. You took the same oath when you accepted your commission in the army and you are now violating that oath, and betraying the trust of your countrymen, by fighting under a faithless tyrant for the destruction of that Constitution and for the ruin of your people's liberties. The perjury and treachery are not *mine*, but *yours*."

The captain indignantly ordered Bowie to shut his mouth. "I shall never shut my mouth for your like," said Bowie, "while I have a tongue to speak." "I will soon relieve you of that," said the captain.

Then he caused four of his minions to hold the sick man, while a fifth, with a sharp knife, split his mouth, cut off his tongue, and threw it upon the pile of dead men. Then, in obedi-

51

ence to a motion of the captain's sword, the four soldiers who held him, lifted the writhing body of the mutilated, bleeding, tortured invalid from his cot, and pitched him alive upon the funeral pile.

At that moment a match was touched to the bodies. The combustible fluid instantly sent up a flame to an amazing height. The sudden generation of a great heat drove all the soldiers back to the wall. The officers, pale as corpses, stood gazing at the immense columns of fire, and trembled from head to foot as if they would break asunder at every joint. Polin stood between them and saw and heard the lieutenant whisper, in a faltering and broken articulation, "It takes him up—to God."

Polin believed that the lieutenant alluded to the ascension, upon the wings of that flame, of Bowie's soul to that God who would surely award due vengeance to his fiendish murderers.

Not being able to fully comprehend the great combustibility of the camphene, Polin also believed that the sudden elevation of that great pillar of fire was an indication of God's hot displeasure toward those torturing murderers. He further believed that the two officers were of the same opinion and thus he accounted for their agitation. And he thought the same idea pervaded the whole detail, as every man appeared to be greatly frightened.

For the time Polin stood amazed, expecting each moment that the earth would open a chasm through which every man in the fort would drop into perdition. Terrified by this conviction, he left the fort as speedily as possible.

On a subsequent day Polin visited the fort again. It was then cleansed and it seemed to be a comfortable place. In the main area he saw the one relic of the great victory—a pile of charred fragments of human bones.[1]

Polin's story, as told by Zuber, makes it quite clear that Bowie was defiant to the end, but Polin does not indicate an

----

[1]Andrew Jackson Sowell, *Rangers and Pioneers of Texas*, San Antonio, 1884, pp. 146-149. Ascribed to the Houston *Daily Post*, March 1, 1882.

attempt on the part of the Texan at forcible resistance. Mrs. Dickinson, the only Texan who survived, told of Bowie's fighting from his bed. She said, "Colonel Bowie was sick in bed, but as the victorious Mexicans entered the room, he killed two of them with his pistols before they pierced him with their sabers."[2]

Dr. John Sutherland, who had been in the Alamo but who had left before the storming of the fort, later heard an account from Mrs. Dickinson which he says was confirmed by Travis's negro boy, Joe. "Colonel Bowie," he says, "being yet sick, was confined to his room, . . . which he had occupied from the beginning of the siege. It was there, while suffering the tortures of disease, unable to lift his head from his pillow, that he was butchered. He was shot several times through the head, his brains spattering upon the wall near his bedside."[3] When the doctor visited the Alamo two years after the battle, he found the marks of Bowie's brains still visible on the wall of the room. According to him, the marks remained there until the wall was finally plastered over.[4]

Doctor Sutherland was interested in Bowie chiefly as a patient—a patient who could not be cured because he suffered from a disease of a "peculiar nature," which "was not to be cured by an ordinary course of treatment."[5] Thus, the doctor might have been somewhat indifferent as to what Bowie did to defend himself against an inevitable death. It seems possible that the phrase, "unable to lift his head from his pillow," may have been figurative.

Then, there was an old Mexican *señora* who thought Bowie suffered from the quite ordinary disease of pneumonia, and she seemed to have a substantial right to her opinion, for as Señora Candelaria told the people of San Antonio for

---

[2]*Ibid.*, p. 141.
[3]Dr. John Sutherland, *The Fall of the Alamo*, San Antonio, 1936, p. 40.
[4]*Ibid.*, footnote, p. 40.
[5]*Ibid.*, pp. 12-13.

years, she had cared for the dying adventurer even after he no longer had any need of care. At the request of Sam Houston, she had abandoned her duties as keeper of a San Antonio hotel to be at Bowie's bedside, but it soon became apparent that her task was hopeless.[6] Two days before Santa Anna's soldiers stormed over the walls of the fort, Jim Bowie died, and Señora Candelaria kept vigil over his body. When the besiegers finally broke into Bowie's room, the woman threw herself across the bed to save the dead man's body from mutilation, but the blood-crazed, victorious soldiers were heedless of restraint, and they wounded her with their bayonets, forcing her back so they could stab again and again the body of their most desperate enemy.

Was that what the old lady really told her friends in San Antonio? Perhaps, but she has time and again been quoted as telling another story—one more nearly in agreement with the accounts given by Mrs. Dickinson and Dr. Sutherland. That story ran something like this:

> I sat by Bowie's side and tried to keep him as composed as possible. He had high fever, and was seized with a fit of coughing every few minutes. Colonel Crockett loaded Bowie's rifle and a pair of pistols and laid them by his side. The Mexicans ran a battery of several guns out on the plaza and instantly began to rain balls against the sandbags.
>
> It was easy to see that they would soon destroy every barricade at the front door, but Crockett assured Bowie that he could stop a whole regiment from entering. I peeped through a window and saw long lines of infantry followed by dragoons filing into the plaza, and I notified Colonel Crockett of the fact. "All right," said he. "Boys, aim well." The words had barely left his lips before a storm of bullets rained against the walls, and the very earth seemed to tremble beneath the feet of Santa Anna's legions.

---

[6]Maurice Elfer, *Madam Candelaria, Unsung Heroine of the Alamo*, Houston, Texas, 1933, p. 8.

The Texans made every shot tell, and the plaza was covered with dead bodies. The assaulting columns recoiled, and I thought that we had them beaten, but hosts of officers could be seen waving their swords and rallying the hesitating and broken columns.

They charged again, and at the time, when a dozen steps from the door, it looked as if they were about to be driven back, so terrible was the fire of the Texans. Those immediately in front of the great door were certainly in the act of retiring, when a column that had come obliquely across the plaza reached the southwest corner of the Alamo, and, bending their bodies, ran under a wall to the door. It looked as though 100 bayonets were thrust into the door at the same time, and a great sheet of flame lit up the Alamo.

Every man at the door fell but Crockett. I could see him struggling at the head of the column, and Bowie raised up and fired his rifle. I saw Crockett fall backward. The enraged Mexicans then streamed into the buildings, firing and yelling like madmen. The place was full of smoke, and the screams of the dying, mingled with the exultant shouts of the victors, made a veritable hell. A dozen or more Mexicans sprang to the room occupied by Colonel Bowie. He emptied his pistols in their faces and killed two of them. I threw myself in front of him and received two bayonets in my body. One passed through my arm and the other through the flesh of my chin. Here, Señor, are the scars; you can see them yet. I implored them not to murder a sick man, but they thrust me out of the way and butchered my friend before my eyes.

All was silent now. The massacre had ended. One hundred and seventy-six of the bravest men the world ever saw had fallen, and not one asked for mercy. I walked out of the cell, and when I stepped on the floor of the Alamo the blood ran into my shoes.[7]

---

[7]*Ibid.*, pp. 16-18. Although Elfer does not include a bibliography in his pamphlet, he cites, in his preface, the San Antonio *Daily Express* of February 11, 1899, and the San Antonio *Light* of February 19, 1899, as his chief sources. A

Thus the señora, in one account, at least, gave credit to the idea that Bowie fought as long as he could. It is a conception widely accepted, as is shown by an article that appeared in *Harper's Magazine* in 1898. The author of the article does not mention the sources from which she got her material, but the story is interesting enough and original enough to justify its inclusion here.

Bowie from his sick bed kept up so desperate a fusillade he built a rampart of dead Mexicans across the doorway of the small chamber where he lay. At last one Mexican more thrust a musket over the barricade of dead men and sent a bullet to Bowie's heart.

Ruthless as they were, Bowie's enemies honored him. Tradition vouches that they buried him apart from the mass of dead, saying, "He was too great a man to sleep with common soldiers." He, himself, would hardly have cared for such sepulture. First and last, he was a man of his people—one with them in aims, in achievements, in passions, errors, and desires.[8]

Although Martha McCullough-Williams does not give credit for her material, and though her version of his death differs slightly from other versions, her account of the disposition of Bowie's body is obviously taken from John J. Bowie's article, "Early Life in the Southwest—The Bowies." John J. Bowie's account follows.

"After the final destruction of all the brave inmates of the Alamo, and when they came to attend to the burial of the dead, tradition says that the Mexican chief officer ordered the remains of James Bowie to be honorably buried by them-

footnote on page 8 explains that his information about Houston's letter to Madam Candelaria was received from James Villanueva, grandson of the lady, who was living in San Antonio in 1933, being connected with the county assessor's office at that time. The narrative is certainly not in the style of a Mexican woman either old or young, educated or uneducated.

[8]Martha McCullough-Williams, "A Man and His Knife, Passages from the Life of James Bowie," *Harper's Magazine*, July, 1898.

selves, as he said, 'he was too great a man to be buried with common soldiers.' He sleeps alone, without any stone or inscription to mark the spot, or to say to the passer-by, 'Here lie the mortal remains of the brave'."[9]

It would have been a suitable tribute for the Mexicans to have paid Bowie, had they buried him with such generous praise and honor as John Bowie envisioned, but such was not the case. All accurate historians have agreed with Polin that the dead of the Alamo were piled up and burned. Such callous disposal might seem an indignity, though it should not, for the burning of bodies by armies is a fairly well established practice. Certainly it is more human than would be lofty and eulogizing speeches. Men do not entertain noble sentiments for dangerous enemies whom they have exterminated. Probably John Bowie described James Bowie's burial as he would have desired it, rather than as it occurred.

The emotions of the Mexicans upon the death of Bowie were probably more nearly like those ascribed to them by Butterfield, who, without citing any authority, says: "Bowie was sick and confined to his cot in a room inside the chapel. He propped himself against the wall as the Mexicans entered, and used his pistols with deadly effect until killed by a bayonet thrust, whereupon the Mexicans hoisted his body onto their bayonets, and carried it triumphantly around the room in an ecstasy of joy at the death of so valiant a foe."[10]

Like Butterfield, Marquis James declares that Bowie "fought from his bed to the last and that his body was pitched about on the bayonets of the soldiers."[11]

Meigs O. Frost, in an interesting and authentic article on

[9]John J. Bowie, "Early Life in the Southwest—The Bowies," *DeBow's Review*, XIII, October, 1852.

[10]Jack C. Butterfield, *Men of the Alamo, Goliad, and San Jacinto*, San Antonio, 1936, p. 12.

[11]Marquis James, *They Had Their Hour*, New York, 1934, p. 138.

57

Bowie, agrees with Butterfield and James, adding an original detail.

"On that cot, unable to stand, Jim Bowie was one of the last five Americans to die. He was still propped up on his cot, knife in hand, two empty pistols on the floor, a rampart of dead Mexicans in front of him, when a Mexican soldier stood in the doorway and shot him.

"His enemies knew him. Drunk with blood, they tossed him on their bayonets 'as farmers with their pitchforks toss hay'."[12]

At least two of the men who died in the Alamo were more widely known to the world than Bowie. Crockett's rough humor and his bear stories had interested the reading public all over the United States. Travis' resolute message from the fort touched the sympathies of the whole western world. Both of these men died as bravely as Bowie, but their deaths did not excite the imaginations of story-tellers more than did that of Bowie. None of the versions of Bowie's death, however, is more dramatic than the manner in which James Bowie's mother received the news of his death.

Bowie's mother, says Walter Worthington Bowie, was a woman of rugged character, endowed with great courage. Once, when her husband had been jailed for killing an adversary in a fair fight, she rode to the jail and, armed with pistols, effected his delivery.

"As indicative of iron nerves possessed by this remarkable woman, it is said that when she was told that her gallant son, James, had been killed by the Mexicans at the Alamo, she received the news calmly, remarking that she would wager no wounds were found in his back."[13]

---

[12]Meigs O. Frost, "Bowie and His Big Knife," *Adventure Magazine*, June 15, 1935.
[13]Walter Worthington Bowie, *The Bowies and Their Kindred*, Washington, 1889, pp. 261-262.

ANECDOTES AS SIDE LIGHTS TO
TEXAS HISTORY

By MARCELLE LIVELY HAMER

I

GEORGE WASHINGTON and the American Revolution are synonymous; yet the traditional anecdote of George Washington, his hatchet, and the cherry tree is more firmly fixed in the American consciousness than the most authentic details of the siege of Valley Forge. To the popular mind a single incident concerning a single individual often stands for a whole people living through a critical epoch. To all but a few specialized historians the history of Scotland over a long period of time resides in the story of how Robert Bruce sat by a cottage hearth to watch some ash cakes cook and was scolded by the peasant's wife for letting them burn. "Assiduous pedantry," in Carlyle's phrase, may dig up and sift "mountains of dead ashes, wreck and burnt bones," constructing history faithful to fact; but unless it is concrete with anecdotes warm and human, that history is not likely to be read, much less remembered.

D. W. C. Baker, as he tells in his Preface, compiled *A Texas Scrap-Book* out of floating recollections and anecdotes connected with history, in order to "embalm the memory of the past." Such materials Judge Alex W. Terrill termed "side lights of history." These "side lights," he wrote — in the face of stern history apologizing to the point of self-contradiction for "the odor of romance"—"reveal conditions of a past era . . . even when destitute of historic value."[1]

Typical of the anecdotes recorded by Judge Terrill and illustrative of Mirabeau B. Lamar's romanticism is one concerning the choice of a site for the capital of Texas:

> General Lamar, in the autumn of 1837 or 1838, weary with official duties, came to the Colorado on a buffalo hunt. After killing all they wanted in the vicinity of Fort Prairie, six miles south of where Austin now is, they were assembled by a bugler on the very hill where now stands the State Capitol building. Lamar, while looking from the hill on the valley covered with wild rye — the mountains up the river, and the charming view to the south, remarked, "This should be the seat of future empire."[2]

Later as President, Lamar directed the commission appointed to select a site for the capital to go to the cabin of Jake Harrell (the only white man living where Austin now is) and look carefully at the location.

These side lights—often out of gossip—on Texas history go back as far as the first exploration. The glowing accounts of Cabeza de Vaca's travels resulted in the expedition of Coronado. Coronado failed to find the Seven Cities of Gold, and in defense of his failure one historian wrote:

> But the witness to whose deposition we are most indebted was Andrés García. This man declared that he had a son-in-law who was a barber, who had shaved the friar after he came back from the new country. The son-in-law told the witness that the friar, while being shaved, had talked about the country which he had discovered beyond the mountains. "After crossing the mountains," the friar said, "there was a river, and many settlements were there, in cities and towns, surrounded by walls with their

---

[1]Alex W. Terrill, "The City of Austin from 1839 to 1865," *Texas Historical Association Quarterly*, XIV (1910), p. 128.
[2]*Ibid.*, p. 113.

gates guarded. They were very wealthy, having silversmiths, and the women wore strings of gold beads and the men girdles of gold and white woolen dresses; and they had sheep and cows and partridges and slaughter-houses and iron forges."

Friar Marcos undoubtedly never wilfully told an untruth about the country of Cíbola, even in a barber's chair.[3]

But to the descendants and followers of those English-speaking pioneers who actually "redeemed Texas from the wilderness" the most significant and interesting anecdotes in history center around the colonists and the characters of the revolution. Stephen F. Austin, the Father of Texas, was not the man to inspire such legions of anecdotes as are still told about Sam Houston. Nevertheless, the following, taken from Baker's *Scrap-Book,* throws a light on the character of some of the settlers and on Austin's attitude towards them that is highly illuminative. Austin, according to the story, sent a census-taker up the Colorado River to take the rolls of whatever people were living in that part of the colony. The census-taker upon his return reported:

"Well, General, to give you a sample of the people living up there. I went to a log cabin where I found only a lady at home. I asked her who lived there. She said, 'I and the old man.' I told her I had come to take the census. She told me to take it. I said to her, 'Have you any children?' She replied, 'Yes, lots on 'em.' 'Please give me their names, madam.' 'Well, thar's Isaiah, and Bill, and Tom, and Jake, and Ed, and John, and Bud, and — oh, yes, I'd like to forgot Joe, he's gone so much.' These being duly noted, with ages, 'Have you no girls?' 'No, sir,' emphatically, 'boys is trouble enough, but arter a while they can take care of themselves.' General, those people are too rough to live with."

---

[3]George Parker Winship, *The Coronado Expedition,* 1540-1542; Extract from the Fourteenth Annual Report of the Bureau of Ethnology, Washington, 1896, pp. 365-366.

Austin replied:

"Those are exactly the people we want for the pioneers on our frontier. They are hardy, honest, and brave. They are not your kid-glove sort. As the settlement becomes denser they will strike farther out upon the borders. I wish we had more of them."[4]

Another incident related by a kinsman of Austin is not unworthy of comparison with the story of Bruce and the spider. Austin, like Bruce, had his discouragements, and like Bruce he succeeded through patient and intelligent effort.

He told me of an incident happening to him on his first trip to Texas, which he said had great influence in forming his disposition in intercourse with others. He said he had with him for the benefit of his party an old hunter, with whom he went out frequently to hunt when the party encamped. The hunter would from time to time caution him to be careful, when he would make a noise treading on leaves or rotten wood. Finally he said to him, "Mr. Austin, you will never make a hunter." "Why?" "Because you need *patience*." Reflecting on this he said to himself: "Here am I on the outset of a great enterprise, and I am told by a faithful person that I can't succeed in a small matter for the want of *patience*; if I am wanting in the ability to do this, how much more will I be wanting in the ability to succeed in my great undertakings? From this day I will devote myself to obtain every requisite necessary for my success. I will *possess patience* and every quality I need." "My friends tell me at times I have too much patience and forbearance, but I think not, for without these, I never should have succeeded in my colonization of Texas." This he writes in his journal afterwards.[5]

---

[4]D. W. C. Baker, *A Texas Scrap-Book*, New York, 1875, p. 311.
[5]Moses Austin Bryan, "Personal Recollections of Stephen F. Austin," *The Texas Magazine*, III (1897), p. 103.

II

The foregoing anecdotes about Stephen F. Austin are taken from printed sources. Long since, he became a subject more for writing than for talk, except in allusion. There are perhaps a hundred printed anecdotes about Sam Houston to one about Austin. This is not at all to argue him a greater man than Austin, though it does show that he appealed more to popular imagination, aroused more interest in his personality, and was more representative of erring humanity. If all the printed anecdotes about Sam Houston were blotted out, a long treatise exemplifying his character could still be constructed from anecdotes told by people in Texas, Tennessee, and elsewhere. According to common report, a goodly number of these living anecdotes could not be printed. Stories stick to Sam Houston as Br'er Rabbit stuck to the Tar-Baby. His capacity for dramatizing himself was unlimited and accounts for many of the stories that survive.

For more than a third of a century Houston lived as a man of mystery, the explanation as to why he left his wife and the governorship of Tennessee being an inexhaustible topic for gossip and for stories created by folk imagination. Houston did not have the wide appeal of Lincoln—another man of mystery—but every facet of his nature had the spark that makes the whole world kin. Any traveler who came to Texas between 1835 and 1865 and wrote of his travels was likely to set down some Sam Houston story he had heard. Reminiscences of Texans who lived during that period are flavored with Houston anecdotes. His friends were loyal; his enemies were bitter; but nobody neglected to talk about him. When the final biography of Houston is written, it will be pungent with anecdotes that go on accumulating.

When the seat of government of the Republic of Texas was moved to Washington on the Brazos in 1842, the boy John

Washington Lockhart laid up a memory of Houston to be recorded many years later. "Having never seen the general before," he wrote,

> I of course watched every movement that he made. I remember him sitting near the edge of the gallery chewing tobacco, and invariably when he would spit he would turn and spit on the floor; but his conversation was so entertaining, his wit and humor so captivating to the large crowd which he invariably drew around him, that this peculiarity was not noticed by anyone save my mother.[6]

Dr. L. L. Click of the University of Texas recalls that in Tennessee at the preparatory school which Sam Houston attended anecdotes are still told of him, the favorite one being how, when he was called before the disciplinary committee for misdemeanors he had committed, he always assumed such an air of injured innocence that he was never punished.

The disorganization and discontent of the Texan army is a well established fact in Texas history. A man with less sympathy than Houston might have failed in command of such an army. To illustrate his way of handling men, one who was in the field with him writes:

> He wished to send a small company of regular troops, over whom his authority was not disputed, back to Goliad to keep up a force at that place. The soldiers objected to going, saying they had been many months in the service, and not received a single cent, and had no shoes to their feet, also were without even soap to wash their clothes. Upon this the general took out his purse, and divided among them all the money he had, amounting to $5.00 each, and refused to take any voucher for the same.[7]

---

[6]Mrs. Jonnie Lockhart Wallis, *Sixty Years on the Brazos*, Los Angeles, 1930, p. 96.

[7]Dr. Joseph E. Field, *Three Years in Texas*, Greenfield, Mass., 1836, p. 26.

64

Another writer to illustrate Houston's sympathetic nature tells how on the retreat to what was to be the victory at San Jacinto, the artillery and baggage wagons mired down continually. Then no man was more willing to clap his "shoulders to the spokes than Old Sam himself. His 'Come on, boys, let's help the poor creatures' became a by-word among the men."[8]

The best anecdotes in the world are character anecdotes, just as the best novels live because of the living characters in them. Many of the best Houston anecdotes not only realize some feature of his character but are "side lights" on the times and society of which he was a part. Perhaps the anecdote to follow is not about Sam Houston but about Pamelia Mann, a noted woman of early day Texas around whom a cycle of legendary yarns has accumulated.[9] The way she took her oxen away from Sam Houston during the Runaway Scrape has various versions, but nobody else had told the story so well as a folk character named Robert Hancock Hunter who was with Houston.

> We were all day a crossing the river, with our wagons, horses & oxen. Then we moved on out Mr Dunahoes, Mrs. Mann, with her two wagons & teams was at Mr. Groces. General Houston got a yoke of oxen from Mrs. Mann to help the cannon a long. (There had ben a greatdel of rain & roads was very bad.) Mrs. Mann said to general Houston, general, if you are going on the Nacogdoches road you can have my oxen, but if you go (the) other to Harrisburg you cant have them, I want them myself. Houston said well I am going the Nacogdoches road but he did not say how far he would go on it. Any how the oxen come & we started. About 6 miles on the road the (roads) forked & the Harrisburg road turned to the right, all most rightangle, down east & and we got about 10 or 12 miles down the road,

---

[8]S. W. Cushing, *Wild Oat Sowings*, New York, 1857, pp. 212-213.
[9]See William Ransom Hogan, "Pamelia Mann: Texas Frontierswoman," *Southwest* Review, XX (1935), pp. 360-370.

and Mrs. Mann, over took us, out on the big prairie hog wallow & full of water, & a very hot day. She rode up (to) the general, & said, general you tole me a d—m lie, you said that (you) was going on the Nacogdoches road sir I want my oxen. Well Mrs. Mann we can't spare them. We cant git our cannon a long with out them. I don't care a d--m for your cannon, I want my oxen. She had a pare of holster pistols on her saddle pummel & a very large knife on her saddle. She turned a round to (the) oxen, & jumpt down with (a) knife & cut the raw hide tug that the chane hook was tide with. The log chane hook was broke & it was tide with raw hide. Nobody said a word. She jumpt on her horse with whipin hand, & way she went in a lope with her oxen.

Capt Rover, (Rohrer) rode up to general Houston, & said general we cant git along with out them oxen. The cannon is don bogged down. Well we have to git a long the best we can. The Capt said, well general I will go and bring them back. He said well. The capt & nother man, started back for the oxen. The Capt got a hundred yeard or so. The general raised up in his saddle, hollowed, Capt Rover (Rohrer) that woman will fite. The Capt said d--m her fiteing. Houston jumpt down of(f) his horse, & said come Boys, les git this cannon out of the mud. The mud was very near over his boot top. He put his shoulder to (the) wheel, & on we went, & got down a bout 6 miles & campt, at big mot of timber. A bout 9 or 10 oclock Capt Rover (Rohrer) came in to camp. He did not bring any oxen. The Boys hollowed out, hai Capt where is your oxen. She would not let me have them. How come your shirt tore so, & some of the Boys would say Mrs. Mann tore it of(f) him. What was that for. She wanted (it) for baby rags. Capt Rover (Rohrer) was our wagon master.[10]

Houston had the reputation of being able to call every man he met by name, whether he had known the man previously

---

[10]Robert Hancock Hunter, *Narrative of Robert Hancock Hunter, 1813-1902*, edited by Beulah Gayle Green, Austin, 1936, pp. 19-21. See also W. B. Dewees, *Letters from an Early Settler of Texas*, Louisville, Kentucky, 1852, pp. 193-194.

or not. His readiness in recognizing individuals certainly contributed to his popularity. Nothing flatters obscurity more than a familiar nod from the great. The way in which Houston prepared to be ready with the name of some stranger is preserved in an anecdote.

In 1839, when between his first and second Presidency of the Republic of Texas he was spending the summer at Nashville, he was riding with a friend out on the Gallatin road on horseback, when they saw a man from Sumner approaching them, on his way to the city, when the General asked who he was. And being told that his name was Hall, and that his brother was killed at the battle of San Jacinto, the General, who had never seen him before, hastened towards him and exclaimed: "How are you, Mr. Hall? I am glad to see you again — how well you are looking." Remembering the General as Governor of the State years before, Mr. Hall expressed his satisfaction at being recognized, and wondered that the General should have remembered him. "Remember you," said Houston, "how can I ever forget you, sir, or any member of your family? Did not your gallant brother die in my arms on the bloody field of San Jacinto?"[11]

Houston was a master in diplomacy, in handling officers as well as rough fighting men. In his personal reminiscences Ashbel Smith relates an anecdote that Texans with an interest in politics tell each other to this day.

San Antonio was much the largest, richest, most influential city of Texas of that period. It was remote from the seat of the Texian government. There was no intervening population between it and the Mexican frontier. For its protection and that of the country, a considerable squadron of cavalry was stationed in that city. This squadron was indeed the only military force of Texas kept mobilized — that was ready to take the field. Major Western, who commanded this body of cavalry, had by some

---

[11]Josephus C. Guild, _Old Times in Tennessee_, Nashville, 1878, pp. 289-290.

acts and significant inuendos intimated that he cared very little for the one-horse government in the city of Houston. President Houston was apprehensive that an order to recall the major or to relieve him might be disobeyed. It was announced publicly that a minister would be appointed to represent Texas at the court of St. James. Colonel William H. Patton was going to San Antonio on his own private business. President Houston, in a long, friendly conversation with Colonel Patton, at length adverted as by accident to the proposed mission to England. He spoke of Major Western, lauded his polished manners, his courtly address, his diplomatic ability—said the major reminded him strongly of Mr. Van Buren — asked Colonel Patton what he thought of the appointment of Major Western to this mission. All this he begged Colonel Patton to hold in strict confidence —"nothing was absolutely determined on"—"Colonel Patton need not be surprised at anything."

The President, waiting till he heard of Colonel Patton's arrival in San Antonio, sent through the War Department orders to Major Western to report in person at the seat of government. The major presented himself in Houston radiant and decorous as Titus at the head of the Roman legions organized for the conquest of Jerusalem. Time rolled on. The major became visibly impatient despite the gracious accord with which President Houston greeted him. At length he began to inquire very quietly who was to be appointed to England — he inquired of your speaker who was a member of Houston's staff — but Ashbel Smith "knew nothing of cabinet matters, he was not a member of the cabinet." Finally, instructions were being made out in the State Department and General Pinckney Henderson was making preparations to leave for London. The rumor leaked out —"the major would not believe it"—"President Houston had better judgment of men"—"what did Henderson know of diplomacy?" The appointment of General Henderson became an established fact. The major "was disgusted"—"he would go back to San Antonio" —and so he did, but he found his successor there well established in command of the cavalry.

68

Referring to this matter at the time, General Houston said to your speaker that he would have no pronunciamentos of the Mexican fashion in Texas during his presidency. During his second presidency he had to confront and ward off the far more perilous danger of two pronunciamentos which were threatened and which might have proved disastrous but for his consummate tact in charming them down. Recurring to the incident just related, General Houston at a subsequent time provided for his disappointed old friend, the major, by placing him at the head of the Indian bureau.[12]

No consideration of Sam Houston as a subject for anecdote would be complete without a story illustrative of his power over a crowd. It amounted almost to magic. His skill in dramatizing himself and the situation was the secret. In the Civil War era, while feeling and vituperation were most intense against him for his opposition to the secession of Texas, he was invited to assist in the military review of a regiment of over one thousand young Texans being drilled at Galveston for service in the Confederate army. The regiment was drawn up for dress parade. Thousands of citizens were assembled. Sam Houston's own son was in the regiment. In the minds of a majority of the Texans present, whether of the military or the civil population, were memories of the bitter campaign that Houston had just gone through. Two of his distinguished opponents, Williamson S. Oldham and Judge Campbell, had been following him up and down and across the state excoriating him on every occasion, during the canvass on secession. Now, the "hero of San Jacinto," dressed in his uniform of 1836, sword at his side, on his head a weather-beaten, light-colored, broad-brimmed planter's hat with the left side buttoned up to the crown, stood out in front of the regiment, supported by the Colonel, in full view of the great gathering of

---

[12]Ashbel Smith, *Reminiscences of the Texas Republic*, Galveston, 1876, pp. 29-31.

69

people. All eyes were upon him—some eyes dim with tears of memory, more eyes dark with premonition of the war to come. General Sam Houston had not spoken a word. Came his first order:

"Shoulder arms."

Order No. 2.—"Right about face." The regiment now facing the rear, the General cried out in stentorian tones of sarcasm: "Do you see anything of Judge Campbell or Williamson S. Oldham there?" "No," was the enthusiastic reply. "Well," said the General, "they are not found at the front, nor even at the rear."

Order No. 3—"Right about, front face."

Order No. 4—"Eyes right. Do you see anything of Judge Campbell's son here?" "No, he has gone to Paris to school," responded the regiment.

Order No. 5—"Eyes left. Do you see anything of young Sam Houston here?" "Yes," was the thrilling response.

Order No. 6—"Eyes front. Do you see anything of old Sam Houston here?" By this time the climax of excitement was reached, and regiment and citizens together responded, in thunder tones, "Yes," and then united in a triple round of three times three and a tiger for the old hero. Thereupon he returned the Colonel his sword, with the remark, "There, Colonel, that will do, I leave you to manage the rest of the maneuvering," and retired from dress parade.[13]

III

Other characters contemporary with Sam Houston in the Texas Revolution would make admirable subjects for biography. A whole company of men impressed their character upon Texas at this time and made Texas what it was. Anglo-American and Scotch-Irish blood gave tone and spirit to the life of Texas. Love of adventure, honesty of purpose, readi-

---

[13]Thomas North, *Five Years in Texas*, Cincinnati, 1871, pp. 95-98.

70

ness of humor, and attachment to politics color the stories of the time. Impatient, impassioned and impetuous the men may have been, but they had the strength and honesty necessary to build a commonwealth. Their forthrightness and sturdiness of character is summed up in a story yet told of Captain King, who was captured with his men near the town of Refugio in March, 1836, the whole band being massacred by order of the Mexican General Urrea.

According to local tradition, when Captain King appeared before the General to receive his sentence of execution, Urrea demanded that King kneel to him. King remained standing and proudly replied, "I kneel to none but God."[14]

These frontiersmen did their own fighting, their own land office work, and their own legislating. As to their ability to do their own fighting, Captain George Erath, one of San Jacinto's heroes, condensed the Texan's whole code of military tactics into one word when he was asked what military training he had had. He replied that he had had none, and added, "I know but vone vord of command, und dot ish, 'Sharge, poys, sharge'."[15]

One of the contemporaries of the time describes Henry Smith, Provisional Governor of Texas in 1835, a salty character who refused to surrender his office when the Executive Council tried to depose him, as follows: "Too illiterate, too little informed, not of the right *calibre* for the station he has been placed in. Organs of self-esteem and combativeness

---

[14]*Souvenir Program, Refugio County Centennial Celebration*, at Refugio, Texas, Wednesday, October 21, 1936. Printed by Refugio *Timely Remarks*, Refugio, Texas, p. 21.

(Some recent historians record that Captain King's name was Amon B. and disregard the old established name of Aaron B. King by which this man was known for a century; but Mr. Tom C. King, State Auditor of Texas, has raised the question and collected data to prove that Aaron B. King is correct rather than Amon B. King, which name the Texas Centennial Commission had placed on several monuments.)

[15]Noah Smithwick, *Evolution of a State*, Austin, 1900, pp. 141-142.

71

large; perceptive faculty good; intellectually small; little reflection or imgination; no reverence."[16]

Illustrative of the character of men and events of the time is a story recorded by Ex-Governor Lubbock in his memoirs.

> Rusk was a grand man. . . . As an illustration of his unremitting toil and energetic action for Texas in the day of her extremity, this anecdote, authenticated by Gov. O. M. Roberts, is told of Rusk:

> "The night of the organization of the government ad interim under Burnet a council was held. Burnet, in a dignified manner, called on one after another for an expression of opinion, coming last to Secretary of War Rusk, who, with his elbows on his knees and his head resting in his hand as if meditating, was actually fast asleep, as he had been at work night and day for three days on the Constitution. Punched in the ribs by the gentleman next to him, he brought himself to the perpendicular and said: 'I think we are in a hell of a fix. We are worked down. Let's go over to the saloon and get a drink, then mount our horses, and go fight like the devil and get out of it.' They went."[17]

Out of the young Republic's financial difficulties has grown an anecdote that is immortal in the chronicles of Texas. At the time of its happening it was a humorous incident; but it ended as a diplomatic issue that is said to have changed the course of Texas history by disrupting negotiations for a loan from the French government. Like all good stories, it has several versions; but its authenticity is established in a document published in 1841 by order of the House of Representatives of the Republic of Texas.[18] A condensed version of the incident is:

---

[16]Colonel William F. Gray, *From Virginia to Texas 1835*, Houston, 1909, p. 111.

[17]Francis Richard Lubbock, *Six Decades in Texas*, edited by C. W. Raines, Austin, 1900, pp. 82-83.

[18]*Correspondence Relative to Difficulties with M. de Saligny, Chargé d'Affaires of France*, by order of House of Representatives, Austin, 1841.

72

In February, 1841, a funny affair occurred, which well nigh caused a rupture of the friendly relation which existed between France and Texas. One of the pigs of Mr. Bullock, an Austin landlord, found his way into the stable of M. de Saligny, the French chargé, and proceeded to appropriate a portion of the corn of the minister's horses. For this offense a servant slew the swinish invader, whereupon the irate landlord horsewhipped the dependent of the French ambassador.

Saligny thereupon complained, and Bullock was arrested and bound over to the next term of court. Afterward the landlord ordered the envoy off his premises. These indignities to French honor were not to be put up with, and the Texas government, failing to give satisfaction, the French minister abandoned his post. A conciliatory letter from President Houston afterward healed the breach and brought the testy Frenchman back.[19]

Another writer in his history of Texas' financial record makes a humorous comment upon the above mentioned incident.

All Texas stood by Mr. Bullock and his pigs. . . . Nor will it be too much to say that, as Rome was saved by the cackling of geese, so Texas was saved by the squeaking of pigs. If the loan had been obtained, it would have been used in establishing a national bank, by which every dollar would have been made to look like ten. The result would have been that the debt of Texas, instead of being twelve millions, would have been twenty-five, thirty, perhaps forty millions. . . . All honor, then, to Mr. Bullock and his pigs; and this heretofore much despised animal must be regarded hereafter as possessed of classic interest. If his figure, carved in marble, should be placed over the entrance of the treasury of Texas, it would serve as a memento to future ages of his having been the salvation of the Republic, and teach Mr. Branch Tanner Archer's "thousands and millions, born and un-

---

[19]D. W. C. Baker, *A Texas Scrap-Book*, New York, 1875, p. 315.

born," that the humblest of agents may be instrumental in producing consequences of the utmost importance.[20]

The incident of a pig's meddling in diplomacy to the extent of changing the current of history may be discounted by earnest historians. It may be disposed of as a mere side light to history. It may not be of enough significance to be treated of as a political event of consequence. But, cemented in print, it long ago became a permanent part of the tradition of Texas. And the historian cannot discount it in his analysis of man and his motives in relation to the events of history.

These side lights to history represent a kind of halfway ground between established historical fact and man's fancy, as exemplified in what "they say." They are the basis for folk tradition, the point where fact and fiction may be fused. The chronicles of Texas are full of such incidents. With a basis in fact they have lived in print; they are source material demanding artistic expression in literature. To use the often quoted phrase, "there is material to burn" for such a literature.

---

[20]William M. Gouge, *The Fiscal History of Texas*, Philadelphia, 1852, p. 111.

THERE'S A GEOGRAPHY OF HUMOROUS ANECDOTES

By *CHARLES F. ARROWOOD*

A STORY is told of Lord Kelvin, the distinguished physicist of the University of Glasgow. I can't vouch for the truth of the tale, but, as it goes, long before he was elevated to the peerage, when he was simply Professor William Thomson, the great scientist was known rather for the significance and profundity of his researches into the field of mathematical physics than for the ease with which his students followed him. It is alleged that in the course of his lectures and demonstrations he was accustomed to leap from one mathematical crag to another, while his students scrambled after as best they could.

Eventually the British sovereign prepared to recognize the great contributions to science of Mr. Thomson by conferring a knighthood upon him. He was, therefore, summoned to the court to receive his honors. During the absence of Professor Thomson from the city of Glasgow his classes were conducted —so the story goes—by a younger colleague named Day. Now, while Mr. Day was by no means so eminent a scholar as Professor Thomson, he did manage to maintain contact with the minds of his students, so that they made splendid progress under his leadership, and liked him very much.

In the meantime events at London moved on their prescribed course; honors were conferred, and one day there appeared on the blackboard of the physics lecture room of the University of Glasgow the following written notice: "On

Tuesday of next week, Sir William Thomson will resume his lectures."

A student who had evidently found the substitute lecturer most acceptable, wrote underneath this notice this quotation: "Work . . . while it is day: the night cometh when no man can work."

Professor Burt, of the Department of Philosophy of Cornell University, tells an anecdote which was a favorite with a friend of his boyhood—an elderly Chinese gentleman.

There lived in a village of China an old grandfather, and with him lived his son and his son's son. The son was a merchant, and so was much away from home. During one of the merchant's absences, the grandfather found it necessary to correct his grandson, which he did—giving him a sound thrashing.

When the son had returned from his travels he learned what had happened: *his* son had been struck, and he—the father—had thus been subjected to the ultimate insult. Such humiliation could not be endured. Arming himself, therefore, with a stout club, the merchant presented himself before his father.

"Father," he said, "I understand that while I was absent you humiliated me by striking my son. I cannot endure such an insult, and will, therefore, strike yours."

So, lifting the club, he thumped himself soundly.

Another story, a favorite with my brother-in-law, Dr. John M. McMillan, of Candor, North Carolina, comes from the Uharrie hills.

Before Carolina was a network of hard-surfaced roads, two youths were taking a walking trip through the Uharries and stopped for the night at an isolated farmhouse. They were made welcome and entertained most graciously.

Now let it be said that in many a rural farm-house of long ago a hole was cut in the door, so that the family cat could

76

come and go at will. The front door of the farm-house where the youths of this story were being entertained was remarkable—it had not one cat-hole, but three.

The boys puzzled about the matter. At length one of them could bear his curiosity no longer. "Sir," he said to his host, "you'll excuse me for mentioning the matter, but do you mind telling me why you have three cat-holes in the one door?"

"I don't mind at all," answered his host. "I have three cats."

"But," inquired the guest, "couldn't all three go out the same hole?"

"Yes," said the host, "they *could;* but when I say 'scat' I mean 'scat'."

Now it is perfectly clear that each of these anecdotes belongs, in a peculiar way, to a particular environment. The story involving Sir William Thomson and Mr. Day belongs to a setting in which higher mathematics, Bible reading, and birthday honors are prominent features—a setting furnished by any one of the four great universities of Scotland. The patriarchal social order of ancient China, with its immemorial etiquette and a system of ethics which invests the filial relation with peculiar sanctity, *makes* the story of the Chinese grandfather, son and grandson; the story would be pointless told of an English family. The Carolina story belongs to a land and a day in which it was no disgrace either to be poor or to be different from other people. The anecdote could have no meaning among people whose first interest it is to learn what is and what is not being done. It's a rural story—a backwoods story, even. These stories illustrate the whole thesis of this paper, that the humorous anecdote, like more pretentious literary forms, roots in the life of a people. If a story is to be understood, it must be studied in relation to the environment which produced it. More important still, persons who aspire to do creative work in the arts and the people who desire to

77

have the arts grow and flourish among them must look to the strength and integrity of their native culture; they must be able to see the cultural resources of their own lives, and to utilize these resources.

An instance of the fashion in which an environment generates humorous anecdotes is furnished by the endless variety of jokes built on some peculiarity of place names. For example, a passenger train of the Illinois Central Railway, northbound, was running through middle Illinois. The train approached the town of Tuscola, and the porter called the station: "Tuscola, Tuscola!"

A little later he called the next stop. "Arcola, Arcola!" he bawled.

A passenger halted him. "Porter," the passenger asked, "is your next station, by any chance, Coca-Cola?"

"No suh," the porter answered, "not Coca-Cola; Champaign."

Such a story doesn't reach very deep into the life of a people; like the pun, its humor grows from simple shock. There are anecdotes, however, which reveal much more of universal human traits and much more of local cultural patterns. The migrating story is of special interest in this connection: such a story migrates because it has a very wide appeal; but if it migrates as a folk story it travels without benefit of glossary or footnotes, and so must achieve intelligibility by becoming a part of every culture in which it is current. Here is an example of a story which has migrated, and has been adapted to a setting very different from that of its origin.

The original is a French folk tale of a peasant who went each week from his native village to his market town, a nearby seaport. His stay-at-home neighbors were accustomed to crowd about him on his return after his weekly trips and to ask him what he had seen at the port. He would then tell them of any-

thing of interest he had learned during the day. On one occasion he had nothing of interest to report, and so had recourse
to invention. He declared that a great wonder had taken place
at the port—an immense fish had appeared off-shore and had
attempted to enter the harbor, but it was of such enormous
size that it could not pass between the head-lands, and so was
wedged in the entrance, completely blocking the channel. The
people for miles around, he added, were crowding the hills
overlooking the harbor in order to see the monster.

This story excited the villagers greatly. Some one exclaimed, "Let *us* go and see this great sight," and ran down
the road toward the seaport. Others followed. The excitement
spread. The inventor of the story watched at first with amuse-
ment and then with consternation. The crowd streamed on—
the village was about to be deserted. The man responsible for
the excitement was himself infected by it. "There must," he
exclaimed, "be something in this story after all." So, catching up his staff, he began to run after the crowd.

This story came to Texas, and took on a Texas character.
A speculator in leases on oil lands—in the vernacular, a lease-
hound—died and went to heaven, only to find the place so
crowded that he could barely find standing room inside the
door. The lease-hound hit upon a trick which he hoped would
relieve the congestion. He produced a scrap of paper and
pencil from his pocket and scribbled the following note, "Oil
discovered in hell," which he dropped on the floor. Presently
the note was picked up and read. The man who read it whispered to a few other persons and slipped away. Those in whom
he had confided similarly whispered to others and followed
him. There was a regular exodus in the direction of the
reported strike.

Watching the procession, the man who had started the
rumor grew more and more restive. At length he could stand

79

it no longer, and muttering, "There may be something in this thing—I guess I'd better look it over," he joined the stampede.

No type of community has been more distinctive of America than has the backwoods; and no American humor is better defined or more robust than the humor of the backwoods. The device most employed by backwoods humor for its effect is exaggeration; but its quality is by no means wholly dependent upon this device. Exaggeration is employed with telling effect because it is used to caricature some distinctive trait or foible.

Take, for example, this story of an Arkansas razorback hog. The razorback has been as distinctive of the southern swamps and pine barrens as the long-horned steer has been of Texas. He was a principal support of life in the region of the Dismal Swamp when Byrd and his party ran the dividing line, and he has been an important economic and social factor in the region ever since. Nothing tougher ever ran on four legs. The razorback may lack the speed of the wolf, the fighting equipment of a wildcat, the strength of a bear, but no wolf, cat or bear can exceed him in ability to absorb punishment and come back for more.

A farmer was clearing a new ground—grubbing up the stumps laboriously, by hand. A county demonstration agent came by and showed him how easily and cheaply the stumps could be removed by the use of dynamite. The farmer was delighted. He went to the store, bought dynamite, fuse, and caps. Coming home, he dug a hole by a big white oak stump, set a charge of dynamite under it, lighted the fuse, and went to his house for supper. The fuse went out, but by that time the farmer was clear of the new ground; so he decided to wait until the next morning before lighting it again.

The next morning, early, the farmer's big razorback hog got up and went foraging. He found that stick of dynamite

80

and ate it. Then he saw the farmer about the barn lot and hustled up to see if he could steal a little corn from the mule's breakfast. He broke into the mule's stall, and made for the feed trough. The mule, naturally, kicked at him, and, for the first and last time in his life, connected. The dynamite, at last, went off.

A neighbor heard the explosion and hurried over. He found the owner leaning over the fence of his barn lot, viewing the ruins.

The neighbor heaved a sympathetic sigh. "It looks pretty bad, friend," he said, "pretty bad."

"Yes," said the victim, "it is bad. Killed my mule, wrecked my barn, broke every window out of one side of my house, and, brother, I've got an awful sick hog."

The housewives of the rural South have long been famous for their hospitality and for the excellence and abundance of the food served on their tables. Some of these housewives, however, never seemed to feel that any meal they served was sufficient in quantity or good enough in quality to be worthy of their guests. They were actually accustomed to apologize for food which was an epicure's delight—to deprecate meals which could not have been better or more lavish. There is a tale which exploits the old theme of a zany in an embarrassing position, which holds the cliché up to ridicule, but which also gives a sly dig at the self-praise of self-deprecation.

A bashful youth was having dinner at the home of some acquaintances. His hostess lamented the fact that she had not known company was coming, and that there was little to set before him.

"Why," said the visitor, "there's plenty of it, such as it is."

Seeing at once that he had said the wrong thing, he hastened

81

to add: "I didn't mean that at all. I do beg your pardon. What I meant to say is, It's fine, what there is of it."

Then realizing he had involved himself hopelessly, he cried in despair: "Oh, I didn't mean that either. I know I must be the biggest fool that ever lived, present company always excepted."

There is an old Carolina story which exploits the theme of pretense exposed, and which employs the familiar technique of the cross-question and crooked answer to elaborate the old saw that he who talks to himself has a fool for an audience. Technique and theme will fit any place or time, but the story draws its color from rural life of an earlier day.

An elderly man was very deaf, was very sensitive about his deafness, and flattered himself that he was able to conceal his infirmity. One day he was building a pig-pen close by the side of the road running through his farm. As he worked, he saw a traveler approaching on horseback.

The deaf man said to himself: "That fellow will ask what I am building. And I'll tell him, 'A pig-pen.' Then he'll say, 'How big are you going to make it on a side?' And I'll say, 'About ten or twelve feet.' Then he'll ask me, 'What'll you take for it when it's finished?' And I'll tell him, 'Fifteen dollars.' He'll say, 'That's too much.' And I'll answer, 'That's what they all say.' Then he'll back out; he'll say, 'I won't give it.' And I'll tell him, 'Well, if you don't, somebody else will.' "

The traveler rode up and stopped. He asked, "What is that place I see across the valley?"

"A pig-pen," said the deaf man.

"How far is it from here?" the horseman then inquired.

"About ten or twelve feet," came the answer.

Puzzled, the rider exclaimed, "What in the name of common sense are you talking about?"

"Fifteen dollars," came the laconic reply.

"You," said the wayfarer, "are certainly the biggest fool I have ever seen."

"That," answered the old man complacently, "is what they all say."

"If," said the traveler, as he gathered up his reins to ride away, "you weren't such an *old* fool, I would take pleasure in punching your head.

"Never mind," the deaf man answered triumphantly, "if you don't, somebody else will."

Politicians and poker are prominent features of the American scene, and no little humor has grown up about them. Here are two stories—one about politicians and poker, the other about a politician. The first is a North Carolina story.

Two men had gone to the Carolina legislature from the mountain region in the western part of the state. One was as close as the proverbial bark on a hickory tree; the other was a waster, who spent a good deal of his time in poker games. The close man lived economically and saved his pay—his *per diem* as he called it—and was generally known to have a good deal of ready cash. The poker player, on the other hand, had a run of bad luck one night, and found himself broke. He approached his fellow mountaineer and tried to make a touch, explaining that he was strapped.

The close man resisted his appeal. "Why ain't you got any money?" he asked. "Ain't you drawing your *per diem* per day?"

"Yes," said the other, "I'm drawing my *per diem* per day, all right, but I ain't drawing my *per noctem* per night."

The story about the politician is from Clarksville, Tennessee.

More than half a century ago a Tennessee politician had angered his Clarksville constituency greatly. In an effort to mend his political fences he was making a speech in a huge tobacco warehouse in the city. The line of defense upon which he relied was a plea that his motives were pure. He had been misunderstood and misrepresented, he claimed. If his constituents could but see his heart, they would understand that he had acted for their good.

In a burst of oratory he grasped the lapels of his frock coat and threw it open. "Oh!" he exclaimed, "that I had a window in my breast, that you might read what is written on my heart! Oh for a window in my breast."

"Mister," yelled a heckler in the back row, "wouldn't a pain in your stomach do?"

Stories of members of various professions or of racial groups change with the changing status or functions of the groups to which they are related. The story of the circuit rider has vanished with the settling of the Methodist ministers as clergymen—the settled minister is a different figure. Stories of the Irish changed as Paddy laid down his pick, and his sons, Pat and Mike, took up the patrolman's night-stick, and they changed again when Pat's son Michael became a contractor. Paddy, of a hundred years ago, faced signs reading, "No Irish need apply," and was the butt of ridicule in stories told of him. Pat and Mike were droll, not ridiculous. Mr. Dooley was our foremost wit and philosopher until eclipsed by that other son of Erin, Charlie McCarthy.

Humor belongs to the soil and air in which it grows.

FOLK CHARACTERS OF THE SHEEP INDUSTRY

By WINNIFRED KUPPER

Illustrations by Ruby Wells

SPAIN gave to the Southwest three animals which have played the major roles in the story of the Southwestern culture. The horse created the Comanche Indian and the cowboy; the long-horn steer furnished a large part of the Texas drama, and the Spanish sheep gave us our two most interesting folk characters—the Mexican *pastor* and the white sheepman. The horse has played his beautiful and spectacular part; the long-horn steer has bawled his last bellow, but the Spanish sheep still occupy the range—and with ever-increasing importance. Since that eventful day when the first Pueblo Indian saw domesticated sheep in Coronado's train, the foreign sheep has been slowly, insidiously, but surely, taking over the ranges. He is the real conqueror of the Southwest.

And for four hundred years the Spanish sheep, chourro and Merino, have been the source of rich but neglected mines of folk-lore and story. For beyond a comparatively few delightful stories of the Mexican *pastores* and some exciting accounts of cattlemen-sheepmen wars, the sheep industry, so important today in Texas and the West, has not yielded a tenth of its possibilities. Of course, wherever Mexican and New Mexican folk-lore has been delved into, the sheep and goat are found, because the sheep industry of the West had its beginning in New Mexico, and with the Spanish and Indian there it played a much more important part than did the cattle industry. The importance of the Mexican *pastor* has been fully acknowledged by such preservers of folk-lore as J. Frank Dobie and Mary Austin, and others. But the *pastor* is just one character in a wide gallery. An old Spanish proverb says that wherever the sheep sets his foot, there the land turns to gold. From this, we get the expression, "the golden hoof." In the Southwest wherever the golden hoof has trod, there are tracks of legend and other forms of lore to be trailed. But if we are to trace the golden hoof, it must be done now; for in a few years it will be too late. When the last of the old sheepmen of the open range is gone, when the last memory of the sheep camp on the great stretches of western lands has died, then there will be closed to us forever a rich, undiscovered story-lode belonging to the Texas scene.

Of all the phases of the story of the early Southwestern sheep industry, the first to consider is the type of folk characters it produced. It is my purpose to write of these characters rather than to relate tales and legends surrounding them.

I. The Anglo-American Sheepherder

This paper will not discuss the Mexican *pastor*, picturesque and important though he is. Instead, since the *pastor's* story has already been told by other and more able commentators, these pages will attempt to portray another representative of the Southwest's sheep range, the sheepman of North European extraction. In popular parlance he is called the *white* sheepman, and for the sake of simplicity this is the term we shall have to use.

In the portrayal of the white sheepman as a folk character we must consider the environmental and historical influences that made him what he was. If this be not within the province of folk-lore, then folk-lore is an ethereal thing with no proper foundation upon which to rest.

Although sheep raising in the Southwest antedates the cattle business by more than a hundred years, the epoch-making industries appear hand in hand, and because of their similarity of condition and purpose no discussion of the one can ignore the other. In introducing the sheep business to the Southwest, the Spaniard carried it on as it had been carried on in his native Spain for centuries, and thus transplanted the folk-ways connected with the sheep-culture of old Spain, which were later to be adopted by sheepmen of another race, for the sheep that were to be raised in the Southwest from that day until this were always to be Spanish sheep and they had to be handled in ways peculiar to their needs and their habits. One of the characteristics of Spanish sheep which was to play a large part in the creation of Southwest story and drama was their tendency to herd in large, compact flocks. Thus was brought to the Southwest the old *transhumante* system of moving large herds to seasonal ranges, a system which had

87

created political unrest and turbulent times in Spanish history, and which was to repeat its history in the new environment. When the cattle kingdom, rising in South Texas, began to push northward under its new American rulers, claiming all the great stretches of free range that it encompassed, it was inevitable that it should clash with the sheep industry in New Mexico and Arizona. The real cause of the sheepman-cattleman war that followed was an economic one, as is the cause of every war; it was competition for the use of a range that belonged to neither contestant. But it had, as every other war, its attendant psychological attitudes, and these attitudes were to determine the general make-up of the early sheepmen of the Southwest.

The sheep business had been a business run by Mexicans and was associated with Mexicans long after the Mexican cattle business had been taken over by American owners. With the cry of *Remember the Alamo* still in their hearts, cattlemen in some sections condemned sheep raising as a business for Mexicans and not for "white men." And they spread their doctrine wherever they took their cattle. "Go into the sheep business?" they would say. "My God, I'm still a white man, I hope. I haven't fallen as low as *that*." Besides, there was the devastating difference that the cowherd worked on a horse and the sheepherder on foot, or when the sheepman—foreman or rustler—did work on a horse, he worked with a slack rein instead of a tight one. This fact that the sheepherder did his work on foot instead of on a dashing cow pony was enough to damn the occupation as unfit for a white man. Tradition has it that you could call a cowboy a thief and he would possibly reply in kind; call him a liar, and unless the time hung heavily on his hands so that he was pining for excitement, you might ride away in safety, though there was no guarantee for this; curse him, and he was likely to express his admiration of your command of invective; but call him a sheepherder, and your blood or his would flow. If you had called him a shepherd, he would not have known what you meant, because there were no shepherds or wool-growers in the early West—just sheepherders and sheepmen. In the early cowboy's estimation there were two classes of human beings, white men and sheepmen, and many a man who toyed with the idea of "fooling with sheep" was loath to face the stigma. In spite of the profits in Merino wool, native Texans, on the whole, would have waited a long time before taking up a business that branded them as an inferior breed of white men in the eyes of their fellows.

It remained for another twist of Fate to augment the number of "white" sheepmen for the Southwest. In the 1880's the immigration movements from England and Germany brought into the Southwest numbers of men who were impervious to social opinion. Many of them were men who had small capital, if any, and were willing to work from the bottom upwards. The western sheep business, the immigration booklets told them, was a poor man's business. A man could apprentice himself, if need be, to another man's flocks, and from his wages soon start out on his own, for the business required little capital—a flock of sheep, a bag of beans, a plug of tobacco. Grass was to be had for the taking, and the mildness of the climate made winter feeding and winter shelter unnecessary. With the investment of three hundred dollars, the booklets read, a fortune could be made in a few years. The picture was irresistible. Men came from over the seas by the hundreds.

So, the man who was to take over a sheep-culture of old Spain, with its attendant Spanish tradition and folk-ways of management, was, in many cases, an immigrant from Northern Europe; and, though by the time of the Civil War there were a number of German sheep men in the hill country of the Guadalupe, the early sheepman was most often a Briton. The immigrant from England and Scotland was easily attracted by a range business familiar to him. The sheep industry of England had for centuries been second only to that of old Spain—with a difference, the difference being that England, because of her low, damp lands, had grown a coarse-wooled sheep, while Spain's sheep had been the finest wooled sheep in the world. Now the fine-wooled sheep from the high, dry lands of Spain had been transplanted to the high, dry lands of the Southwest, and here two great sheep cultures met—the Spanish sheep with the British sheepman; and Texas was to develop the Southwest's most interesting character, the Anglo-American sheepman.

Where the black condemnation of the sheepman was something that the ordinary man could not face, it held no terror for the Englishman. Safe in the consciousness that he *was* an Englishman and, therefore, in his own mind, superior to anybody else on earth, he could indulge with impunity in an occupation conceded to be lower than any other on earth, because, after all, was he not an Englishman, and didn't he feel a tinge of pity for anyone who wasn't, even though that one be a lordly cattle king? The fact that in Texas the intelligence of the sheepherder was rated lower than that of the mule and the jackrabbit deterred him not a whit, even if it was necessary for him to start at the bottom. He came to the Southwest, he raised sheep, he made good, and he was happy enough the while, for was he not an Englishman?

And he often started as a sheepherder, competing successfully with the Mexican *pastor,* because the white man owner understood how to get along with him better than with the unfamiliar type of Mexican laborer. He usually promoted himself to the role of manager of flocks, called rustler, majordomo, caporal, or foreman, and from this position he often became owner of flocks—a sheepman in his own right. So the term *sheepman* can apply to a man in any one of these stages,

90

This is <u>NOT</u> a West Tex.
Sheepherder

because the early sheepman usually went through all three of them.

This self-promotion of the western sheepherder is one of the many factors that differentiates him from the shepherd of the old world. The old-world shepherd, like the Mexican *pastor*, remained a shepherd throughout his life. Perhaps the fact that he never grew above his picturesque state accounts for the vast amount of literature devoted to him. For two thousand

91

years and more the old-world shepherd was a gentle tender of flocks, a singer of songs, a lowly, humble, placid servitor, the representative of all that was quiet and peaceful in pastoral life, literature and painting. Not so his American brother. His life was more virile, more adventurous by far. He could not have led a quiet, idyllic life if he had wanted to, and the obstacles he had to face kept him from attaining the colorless character that is ascribed to the old-world shepherd. One writer reminds us that in the old world, when people saw the shepherd of earlier times appearing over the hills in the sunset glow, they cried, "Lo, behold, the gentle shepherd cometh," whereas, in western America they greet him with, "Well, look at that lousy sheepherding scoundrel coming over the divide with his damned sheep. Boys, get your black masks and the wagon spokes." With such an animosity to face, any man could develop into an interesting character.

The sheepherder had to be intelligent, too. He had two thousand sheep for which he was responsible; and two thousand fleeces on the hoof could not be trusted to the care of nit-wits. He had to be intelligent, loyal to a trust, not averse to hard labor, and willing to live alone. When he became a rustler, or foreman, he was responsible for two or more flocks of two thousand, each with its herder, and it was his job to find suitable range, get supplies to his herders, and arrange for shearing, lambing, and getting the flocks to market. This intelligence of the sheepherder and the rustler was one of their salient characteristics. One feels compelled to suggest, with more or less delicacy, that this characteristic of intelligence and maturity is one of the marked differences between the cowboy and the white sheepherder. For a difference there was, and it was not so much due to the fact that one worked with cows and the other with sheep.

It was the set-up of the individual that determined the occupation. The sort of man who made a good cowboy would not necessarily have been a good sheepherder. Cowboys were men who craved action, and had little use for anything else. If we are to rely on the many pictures that have been drawn of this character, we get the impression that he was, to use John Clay's words, "a devil-may-care, roystering, gambling, immoral, revolver-heeled, brazen, light-fingered lot, who usually came to no good end." But sober-minded people would hesitate to accept such a wholesale denunciation of a group of individuals who have proved themselves essentially harmless, particularly when the denunciation comes from a man like Clay, who was chiefly interested in finding docile labor content to eat bacon. The worst that should be said, in the interest of truth, about the old-time cowboy is that he was the perennial adolescent of the range. Typically he was a boy in his twenties—a Peter Pan of the Southwest. His work required the action, danger, and spectacular skill that the adolescent dreams of; his recreation was as boisterous and as care-free and as careless as that of any small boy; his songs were the innocuous words and the simple rhythm of a Mother Goose jingle; his stories were the tall tales reminiscent of dragon and giant legends; his costume was the colorful gaudiness of eternal youth.

In contrast, the sheepherder, as well as the rustler, had to be a mature individual. The aloneness of his life, with days, weeks, and months spent with only the sheep, the coyotes, his dog, and himself for company, necessitated his being a man of intelligence with rich resources within himself, or else a man of so little intelligence that he could not notice his loneliness—and this last type was rare, because it could hardly be trusted with money on the hoof. A man possessed of mentality at any state between these two could not cope with such a life. If he tried it, he was, according to many commentators, likely to go insane. This loneliness of a sheepherder's life is often the theme of those who write without

93

actually experiencing the life themselves. The sheepherders who have written of their own experiences, such as Chapman and Gilfillan, fail to mention it.

The western term, "crazy as a sheepherder," is supposed to have originated from this idea that the loneliness of his life actually drove the sheepherder crazy, but the real origin of this familiar term was probably the cowboy's lack of understanding of the sheepherder. It is the same lack of understanding that exists between boisterous adolescence and philosophic maturity. For one thing, the white sheepherder was very apt to spend his long periods of inactivity in reading, an occupation that the average cowboy could in no wise understand. One of the several characteristics upon which all writers on the sheepherder agree is this propensity to read. His reading matter varied from months-old periodicals and newspapers to Shakespeare.

It was not always the inactivity of the job that made him read, however. It was, rather, as has been said, that the sheepherder was naturally the type of man who would choose reading as a recreation. Whatever it was that made him read, he did read, and reading does things to a man's personality. His reading brought thoughts, his thoughts ran into grooves of philosophy, his philosophy cropped out in his speech, or kept him speechless, and all this made him wholly unintelligible to the cowboy.

Unlike the cowboy, the sheepherder created few folksongs. What could a man who read Shakespeare and the *Illustrated London News* contribute to

> Come ti yi yoopee,
> Ti yi ya!

Or perhaps that was his loss. Nor did his contemplative nature find joy in tall tales, though he was not above letting his reading matter furnish other people's tall tales for his practical use. There are several sheepherder legends that

94

illustrate this, but one of them is a true story of the experience of M. H. Kilgore, sheepman, as told by Florence Angermiller in the Uvalde (Texas) *Leader News*. Mr. Kilgore had an encounter with a cattleman in the Big Bend country about 1887. The cowman had sworn to kill anybody who ever came in there with sheep, and though Kilgore had a lease and a right to be there, it didn't count much against the cowman's guns. After he had located his sheep at Rosillo Springs, a delegation of three cowpunchers rode up and wanted to know what he was doing in there with sheep. He saw he was outnumbered; so he resorted to the usual sheepman policy of strategem. He had been reading about Jules Verne's trip to the moon; now he began to paraphrase it for the cowboys. He told them that his partner and he had constructed a machine for the trip, and that they had got it loaded with ballast, water and supplies, and since they couldn't leave the faithful old sheepdog, they had put him inside, too. They had risen to about 5,000 feet and were traveling at a fair rate when they had discovered at midnight that they were losing altitude. They began throwing out ballast, and still losing altitude, they went to throwing out other things, until finally, in desperation, they threw out the old sheepdog. They traveled without difficulty after that, and at daylight they looked out to discover that the dog, faithful to his trust, was traveling right along beside them in the air. When he got to this point, the leader of the cowboys got up hurriedly and said to the others, "This damned fool is crazy. Let's get out of here." And from then on that bit of range belonged to Mr. Kilgore.

Besides the fact that the white sheepherder was a mature individual, a heavy reader, and often a Briton, he had another characteristic which all commentators agree upon. This was the general unattractiveness of his appearance. Here is another contrast to the cowboy, for, while the cowboy was at times a picture in expensive regalia, the sheepherder rarely took the trouble to adorn his person, even for the public eye. The exigencies of his job called for no more picturesque equipment than a sling shot, which was handed down to him from the Spanish shepherds, or a curved stick, a sort of a boomerang with which the Navajo Indians had been killing rabbits for centuries and which they quickly adapted to the new business of herding sheep. Add to these two bits of equipment, a canteen, a canvas satchel containing a midday lunch, a pocket-size book, a pipe, and an important trio composed of a piece of punk, a piece of steel, and a flint rock which, together, formed the cigarette lighter of the open range, and you have the sum total of the sheepherder's necessary equipment. There was nothing in these pieces of commonplace properties to dress up to. Perhaps the best account of a sheepherder's typical appearance is that given by Robert Maudslay, sheepman, in the unpublished chronicle of his life on the open range. He describes himself as a sheepherder:

> You see, then, a young man of about thirty-four with a beard several inches long, hair sadly in need of a cut, though there were unmistakable signs of a rude attempt to cut said hair, which looked as though the possessor had attempted to be his own barber. He had. And the method was the most primitive on record, and a very simple one. He had no mirror, and he proceeded with his tonsorial work entirely by touch. There was a family comb with some teeth missing, a family hairbrush the color of which was much in doubt, though it looked black enough to be really black; there was a family towel, several in fact, that had served at one time as containers of oats. For his hair-cutting the family comb and a pair of sheepshears were all the tools he needed; quite often he dispensed with the comb and used only the shears. This tonsorial artist would first proceed to some secluded spot in order to avoid

any intrusion; then he would run the fingers of his left hand through his hair and cut with his right all the hair, irrespective of where it grew, that protruded above them. Having thus proceded over the entire area of his head, he would emerge from his retirement to enjoy that delightful feeling of coolness that a hair-cut is supposed to give. Once, when I actually went to a barber (he was a Mexican), he looked at me reproachfully and said, "Your hair no cut by barber."

My shoes were of the style known as *O. K.'s*. Nails covered the bottom, and the uppers were fastened with a buckle such as you sometimes see on leggings. My shoes were always run down so much on one side that the uppers were constantly threatening to become the lowers, and the soles seemed always to be aspiring to become uppers on the opposite side. In fact, a casual glance would suggest a game of round-about between them. Sometimes when I was assailed by a fit of economy, I would change the feet and use the right shoe on the left foot and vice versa. Then my shoes would look like a shapeless mass of leather that had been in a mangle, and my Mexican barber would have said, "Your shoes no made by shoemaker." I remember that at one time I was herding a flock close to the road in Howard Canyon when I saw a man on the road coming towards me. I was almost barefoot at this time, and when he told me that he was on his way to town and was intending to buy himself a completely new rig, since he'd been in the woods all winter, I glanced casually at his boots. They were in fairly good shape and apparently about my own size.

So I said, "If you are going to town, why not trade your boots for mine, and I'll give you a dollar to boot."

This seemed to strike him favorably; so he dismounted to take off his boots. "You're on," he said cheerfully, and gave me the boots. Then he looked critically at mine, turned them over and looked again, and then threw them away. He went off barefooted, and I stepped out joyfully in my new acquisitions.

Then there were my stockings. Sometimes they were stockings and sometimes a piece of an oat sack wrapped around my feet;

97

I really preferred the latter, because all my stockings proper had holes in them and it was sometimes confusing to find which hole to put my foot through. It really didn't matter which hole I used, because my feet would come out again in some other place anyway.

My pants, excepting for a period just after they were bought, were picturesque. They were always the exact color of all the bare ground around me. But if they didn't have much color, they did have many patches, and to my honor be it said that the patches were nearly always in front. I employed a sort of system, too, in the regulation of my pants. If a button was missing, it was immediately replaced by a mesquite thorn. We hadn't any pins, that is, metal ones; all ours grew on trees. You have no idea what a variety of uses a mesquite thorn can be put to. I once skinned and cleaned an antelope with one. But to the pants. A casual rent in them could be quickly repaired with a thorn, but there always came a time when a patch became imperative, and this I would accomplish with a needle and thread and a piece from a discarded pair. I employed system in this, too. If the patch wore out, I would patch the patch, and if that wore out, I would even sometimes patch the patched patch, but I never under any circumstances allowed myself to go further than this and patch the patch that patched the patch. No, sir! I'd sunk pretty low, but not so low as all that. I would magnanimously throw them away. There was a limit to my degradation.

My undershirt? I must confide to you, *sub rosa,* that I hadn't any. In the winter time I used to double up and make my summer top garments become the under garments for winter use.

As for my hat, really it was more than a hat; it was two hats. And each of them was in a different stage of antiquity. One of them was minus a brim and the other minus a crown, but the two together formed a fairly complete head covering. If they had both been of the same color it would not have looked unusual in any marked degree, but one of them was black, and the other had been white. I would hardly know how to diagnose the color as it was then, except negatively—it was not black.

All this, with a canteen slung across my shoulder, a rifle resting in the hollow of my left arm, a curved stick in my right hand, is a pretty accurate picture of me as I contemplated paying my people a visit. When I thought back upon myself as I had been several years before this, I could see a fellow on a Manchester street, trigly dressed, his linen immaculate, his hat an impeccable derby, and cane in the crook of his arm instead of a rifle, and a correctly gloved hand raised to summon a cab. But I wasn't interested in him; I liked better this other me who now weighed a good solid one hundred and fifty-five pounds, was as suntanned and as weather-stained as anybody could well be, and who felt stronger and more fit than he'd ever done in his life. I could lift a sack of salt weighing two hundred pounds and put it into a wagon alone; and once I threw two thousand sheep of all sizes into a vat in five or six hours without aid from anyone. I had no desire to return to the identity of the fellow on the Manchester street.

Often the legends of the early sheepman center on this theme of disreputable appearance. Wherever sheepmen of those days are talked of, the name of John M. Shannon of San Angelo crops up sooner or later. Old Man Shannon he is called, and legends have fallen thick around his name. There is the story of the man who accosted him on the streets of San Angelo one day and reproved him for his careless appearance. "Look here, Mr. Shannon," he said, "you're a millionaire now. Why do you still go around looking like a sheepherder? Look at you, no socks, sloppy old pants, greasy hat. Why don't you *dress* like a man that owns two banks?"

"Aw," replied Old Man Shannon, "don't have to. Everybody knows who I am here. Don't have to dress to show what I've got."

A few months after this encounter the same man met Old Man Shannon on the streets of St. Louis — same sockless state, same sloppy pants and greasy hat.

"Now, see here," he expostulated, "you're in a big city now, Mr. Shannon. You ought not to be seen like that."

"Aw," said Old Man Shannon, "nobody knows who I am here. Why not?"

Another legend of Old Man Shannon, the millionaire sheepman, has at least half a dozen versions. Perhaps the best one is the one Mr. Marvin Hunter tells. A sheep buyer, goes the story, was going toward the immense Shannon ranch to buy some fine-blooded rams. Near the Shannon ranch he came across the shack of one of the ranch workers. He knew the ranch house itself was a good distance farther on. He was thirsty, so he stopped for a drink. An untidy old fellow was standing at the gate watching him as he climbed down from his buggy, and when the buyer asked if he could have a drink, he said, "Reckon so, just go in and ask for it."

"Mind holding my horse for me, then?" the buyer asked.

"Nope, not a bit," he answered.

The stranger got his drink, climbed back into his buggy, gathered up the reins and threw the old fellow half a dollar.

"Now," he said, "know anything about those rams Old Man Shannon has for sale? Are they any good, or is the old boy just lying?"

"Finest rams in the world," the man told him.

"How do you know? Do you work for Shannon?"

"I sure do. I'm Old Man Shannon myself."

The discomfited buyer apologized profusely for having had the bad taste to give Mr. Shannon a fifty-cent tip, but Old Man Shannon said, "Not at all, not at all, easiest half dollar I ever made."

And he carefully pocketed it.

But if the sheepherder didn't look like the cowboy, he

100

could swear as hard, play as good game of poker, and drink as much, on the rare occasions when he came to town, though he rarely made as much noise. Who, says Mary Austin, has ever heard of a sheepherder painting the town red? Who, ask we, has ever heard of any philosopher painting any town red? Certainly it was not moral compunction that kept him from red paint, for, like the cowboy, he had little of the Puritan in him. The care of two thousand exasperating, silly sheep, and the hours of meditation thereon are not factors calculated to produce Sunday school superintendents. In a land where every man was an individualist living a life of individual ethics, the sheepman was supremely individualistic. He was forced by circumstance to formulate, consciously or unconsciously, a personal code which served him and his environment, and which, fitting for the great open spaces of the West, had no room for dogma.

The sheepman of the open range was an individualist. He was more. He was a creature peculiar to a certain phase of range history. There was nobody exactly like him in all the wide stretches of the West, and as one type that contributed to the making of western history, he is important.

In *Scribner's Magazine* for January, 1909, there appears a painting of the Southwestern sheepherder by the artist N. C. Wyeth. He has given us a man—rugged, tattered, alone under the stars, with his sleeping flock, a watchful dog, a dying fire; in one roughened hand a well-worn pipe, in the other an open book—the ever-present book. But the man is staring into the fire, thinking. No more accurate picture than this can be given, no matter what the medium.

II. The Foreman and His Long Drive

A little above the sheepherder in respectability, and therefore a little lower in picturesqueness, was the man whose business it was to direct the sheepherder's work. As has been

said, in New Mexico and along the border he was *caporal,
vaciero, major domo;* in the more direct language of West
Texas he was often called *rustler,* a term which must not
be confused with the same term used in connection with the
cattle business; but to the sober writers on the technicalities
of sheep-raising he was simply a *foreman.*

The rustler, unlike the herder, did his work on a horse,
but the horse rarely had the dash of the contemporary cow-
pony. It did not need to have. There was no spectacular cutting and running to be done. In fact, there was little
that was spectacular about the work of the rustler. He had
eight thousand sheep or more under his care, and he was
responsible to his boss, who was either an individual who
often carried on other businesses while he left the sheep-
raising to his rustler, or a corporation, such as Swift and
Company, who employed many foremen to buy and bring
their stuff to market. But with all his responsibility, his life
was a comparatively quiet one, even though it had elements
of activity unknown to the herder.

The rustler's hardest work came on the long drives that
were a part of the sheepman's experience in the days of the
open range and that furnished most of the drama in the life
of the early sheepman. These drives covered thousands of
miles. Huge herds, often of twenty thousand sheep, were
grazed from California across Arizona and New Mexico to
Texas, and from California through Nevada and Utah to
Wyoming, or from Idaho and Montana down through Colorado to Texas. If sheepmen had been disposed to tell tall
tales, here was their opportunity. The long sheep drive to
market was of much longer duration than the long cattle
drives and fuller of incident. There were, in the earlier drives,
the constant brushes with Indians, as on the drive from New
Mexico to California with nine thousand sheep, in 1852,
described by H. L. Conrad in his *Uncle Dick Wooton.* There

102

were in later days the disagreeable and often dangerous contacts with cattlemen and homesteaders, and the difficulties with the irate inspectors of different states. There were always the caprices of the weather, which necessitated the digging of sheep out of snow in the northern states and the hunting of water in the southern states. Yet out of all the faithful accounts given, there is no attempt to enlarge the difficulties. Few legends grew here of a sheepman's making; and, because of the comparatively short period over which these drives took place — the period between 1850 and the coming of the railroads — few traditional folk-ways pertaining to the sheep-drives can be said to have developed. There were certain characteristics typical of all drives, it is true, such as the inevitable trouble each foreman had with the men he had to employ on these drives. (The long drive was the responsibility of the rustler, or foreman; the experienced sheepherders were rarely spared to leave the home range. The driving crew usually consisted of adventurers seeking a change, outlaws seeking escape, and befuddled Mexicans who, knowing nothing of geography, would start out in good faith, but, becoming frightened at the distance separating them from their homes, would usually quit after the first few days.) However, the characteristics of the long drives, and the events that occurred along their course, are properly matters for history rather than folk-lore.

Another story quoted by Miss Angermiller from W. H. Kilgore, in the Uvalde *Leader News*, has all the possibilities of a bit of legend in the making. Mr. Kilgore was having the usual labor trouble on one of his sheep drives but was fortunate in discovering at least one reliable driver. He had a pack pony that learned to work behind the sheep and nose them on.

When we would get into prickly pear, the sheep would be almost impossible to drive. They would get to eating pear and you couldn't budge them. Old Pack caught on that they wouldn't go unless they got scared, so he would stop, then suddenly give his pack a genuine good shaking. Those tin cans and skillets rattling would stampede the sheep every time and away they would go. If a horse ever laughed, Old Pack did. He would stand there and watch them and it looked like he got the most pleasure out of the little stampede he caused.

One tale that grew out of a sheep drive became widespread into various versions. Robert Maudslay claims to have made it up out of an idle mind from experiences with deceitful distances and narrow rivers he encountered on his long drives. When this story was last seen in print it was in the book *Sheep,* by Archer B. Gilfillan, published in 1929. Mr. Maudslay gives the following account of its genesis:

From this point we started towards Cheyenne, and on the way we passed a number of streams dignified by the name of rivers. One of them, called Spring River, was about three feet deep, and here I accomplished the impossible feat of crossing a river three feet deep without any kind of a bridge and without wetting any part of the wheels of the wagon or the horses' feet. The banks of this narrow river were overgrown with a very thick, coarse grass which bent over the stream and which had probably, in the course of growing, accumulated and held quite a lot of loose soil blown there by the wind. At any rate, this dirt-laden grass formed a firm bridge which bent over the stream with a gap at the top of not more than eight inches, and although there was a rushing stream two feet below it, all the driver had to do was to induce the horses to step over this narrow gap, and the trick was done.

It was this river that inspired the making of a little story to use in illustrating how deceptive the distances are in the clear air of this country. The now nearly worn-out joke runs something like this:

A stranger to the country was visitor for a few days in a sheep camp, and seeing a mountain which appeared to him not more than a mile or two away, he told his host that he would walk to it and back again to gain an appetite for breakfast. The sheepman let him go without undeceiving him; so the man started and steadily walked till noon, but he found himself very little nearer the mountain. He had by this time reached the banks of one of these deep but narrow streams and paused in his walk. It looked too deep to wade, so he began to strip off his clothing. A native of the place happened to see him and asked what he was stripping for.

"To swim across the river, of course," he answered.

"Lord, you don't need to strip for that; you can just step across it."

"You can't fool me with any such talk as that. You see that hill over there? Well, I've been walking toward it for five hours and I haven't got any nearer; so I'm sure that on the same basis this river is at least twenty miles wide, and I'm going to swim it."

It was I who originated this poor joke. I conceived it at the time I crossed that strange river, and I told it to my men at the time, but after several years the story was told to me more than once, and with little variation, and I felt as I imagine the father of the prodigal son felt.

There are many tales told by sheepmen of their long drives, some of them comic, some tragic, others merely exciting, but they are for the most part accounts of actual events and could hardly be classed as folk legends, at least not at this early date. All of these stories belong to the first part of the sheep-raising era, for as farms grew and wire fences spread, the sheep were transported by rail, and the institution of the long drive became a thing of the picturesque past.

III. LEAD GOATS

Among the folk characters peculiar to the sheep industry is that individual that became indispensable when the railroads came to the sheep country — the lead goat. Goats had been used on some of the long drives. They had been used by the Navajo herders before the advent of the white sheepherder. The Navajos and the Mexicans in New Mexico had used them as part of their camp equipment — a source of milk supply. No doubt these early herders soon discovered the propensity of these adventurous animals for leading the rest of the flock across streams and into pens. When the railroads came and the difficulty of getting sheep into cars arose, the lead goat was resorted to as a means of enticing the unwilling sheep to their doom. Again Robert Maudslay may be quoted:

> In loading sheep a trained sheep or goat is generally used. This old deceiver is placed in a pen where the correct number of sheep for a single deck are held, and at a given word, the gate is opened and the old fraud will indicate in a way well understood by the dupes around him, "Come on, let's get out of here," and they follow him right into the car. This wily old-timer will stay at the far end of the car until the last one is in, and then he will sneak out at the car door and work his wiles on another bunch. He is remorseless, and the utter ruin of thousands of sheep-lives—a veritable Pied Piper of Sheepdom.

It soon became apparent that there were lead goats — and lead goats. Especially proficient Pied Pipers became fixtures at railroad stockyards and were often treated as temperamental *artistes*. Their individualities were usually honored by nick-names, and they were sources of tales that spread through the sheep country they served. The following story by Colonel Jack Potter appeared under the title "The Dissipating Lead Goat" in the *Union County Leader* of Clayton, New Mexico:

Back in the early days when the Colorado and Southern railroad built through this country and established shipping points up and down their line, old-time pioneer sheep and cowmen could hardly get used to this modern way of handling livestock —shipping, not driving. . . .

When it came time for the first big shipment to be loaded out, the wild range sheep were not used to corrals or shipping pens. Even their . . . lead goats failed to function when they were supposed to lead the sheep into stock cars, especially the second deck to which the leading chute was much higher than the lower. . . .

By doing a little research work the C. & S. soon found a gentle goat that would lead up and through both decks for hours at a time, and he became so prominent that the boys insisted on naming him for some big sheep man or boss.

Most everyone had selected a name for the lead goat. At first it was suggested naming him Bob Dean; next, Jim Carter; third, Sol Floersheim; and last of all, Horace Abbot. The name Horace Abbot fitted in because Abbot was the only one in the group that had chin whiskers that matched the goat's. . . .

At this time there was a tramp or handy man named Timbuck doing odd jobs around town and sleeping in a stall in the livery stable. He and Horace Abbott had adjoining stalls and became great pals. . . .

In the busy shipping season Timbuck would be employed to help load out, and many a day you could see Timbuck and Horace Abbot start for the yards early and return late. Timbuck, after a day's work, would take home a pint of whiskey, which he called his wake-up tonic.

He had taught Horace Abbot to drink out of a bottle. . . . The goat learned how to chew tobacco and kept on dissipating. Many a night he would hang around the back door of the saloon,

108

waiting for Timbuck, and they would start home in the darkness, both of them pretty well stewed.

Finally the shipping increased and Timbuck and Horace Abbot fixed up an old box car on the stock yards siding, and ate and slept in it. After a hard day's work they would come down town to the Favorite Saloon, Timbuck never taking a drink without taking one out to Horace Abbot. They would leave late in the evening, with Timbuck leaning on Abbot, for their home in the box car.

One day an order came down the line from the dispatcher's office at Trinidad, giving orders for No. 19 to pick up all the empties on the siding at Clayton. Well, that night the car that was used as a home by Timbuck and Horace Abbot was attached to No. 19, very likely unbeknown to the loving friends inside. No doubt after this nocturnal ride, they awakened in some greener field. When it was discovered that they were really gone, one old wise hombre out of a group said, "Clayton has lost a good citizen and a fine lead goat."

Later many rumors came in. One was that they had arrived at Pueblo, and that Timbuck went into the mountains to prospect and that the C. & S. had given Horace Abbot the Keely treatment and was using him as a leader in stock yards and packing houses.

IV. THE SHEEP DOG

No discussion of the sheep industry's folk characters can be carried far without mention of another worker with the flock, the sheepherder's dog. Stories of the remarkable feats of the Southwest's sheep-dog must some day be brought together into volumes. When this is done, it will be found that of all the stories of the open range, those containing the greatest drama of courage, bravery, and perseverance will not be those of the buffalo hunter, the trapper, the cowpuncher, or the sheepherder, but of the sheep-herding dog. These stories are told by every sheep owner, rustler, or herder

109

who used a dog. The best of them are to be gleaned from the Mexican *pastores,* who were the most adept in the training and using of their dogs. The tales themselves are usually short bits, relating the dog's general traits and his marvelous genius. To attempt an adequate recital here is useless. Besides, the purpose of these pages is to account for folk characters, rather than to present legends.

The sheep-dog, called shepherd dog in the East, and *pastor* dog by the Mexicans, belonged to both the Spanish and the British sheep cultures. The management and training were much the same everywhere, but necessarily differed in the respect that the English sheep grazed loosely in pastures and did not herd together in compact bunches, while the Spanish sheep were essentially herd-sheep, and therefore were less individualistic — if any sheep can claim to be less than scarcely individualistic at all. The English shepherd dog, then, and the Spanish shepherd dog had different jobs. But it is doubtful that there was much difference in their efficiency when trained from the first for range sheep.

Most of this training was old-world training, with one new element added to fit the new environment. In the vast stretches of the Western plains the sheep-herding dog had to be taught sign language. His master at times had to give directions from a distance greater than his voice could carry. He could do this with the well-trained dog by means of a system of arm movements that the dog readily understood.

The duties of the dog were two-fold. He had to be able to keep his sheep within the flock during the day, and after sundown he was supposed to sound a warning of nightly enemies, standing ready to defend the flock with his life, if necessary.

Such reliability as was required of the sheep-dog could come only with the most careful training; and in the training of the dog no man who ever worked with sheep was

more successful than the Mexican *pastor,* whose methods
have been described by J. Frank Dobie in his *Tongues of
the Monte:*

> To make a true *pastor* dog, the Mexican takes a pup before
> its eyes are well opened and delivers him to a nanny goat from
> which her new born kids have been removed. At first she must
> be held and forced to allow the puppy to suck. . . . He grows
> up thinking he is a goat, but at the same time asserting his
> canine antagonism for coyotes and other predatory animals.
> He not only protects the goats but learns to keep them together
> and to direct their course. He seldom barks, going about his
> business quietly.

The early *pastor,* who was *partidario* rather than a hireling,
saw to it that his dog was trained to act as a complement
to his own herding. Thus the dog was invaluable to him.
Indeed, it is said of the Mexican sheepherder that he would
sigh if he lost a friend and groan when his wife died; but
that if death took his favorite dog, his grief was manifested
in an overwhelming anguish that refused to be consoled.

But when the Mexican sheepherder became the hireling
for the white sheep owner, the story changed tone; and the
meeting of the two sheep cultures brings forth what is probably the first record of adverse criticism of the shepherd
dog. For we find reports from the white sheepmen that the
pastor's dog, instead of walking like a faithful sentinel on
the outer side of the flock and quietly leading the strays
back by their ears, was often allowed to "dog" the sheep,
that is, to worry them unnecessarily, while the sheepherder,
in order to save his own feet, relied too much on those of
his dog. This, however, seems to be the opinion of a minority,
and what lack of respect the sheep-dog has suffered may be
attributed to the lack of respect the Anglo-American sheepmen had for the Mexican herders. The sheep were Mexican

111

and Spanish, and their herding was necessarily done after the Spanish custom. In understanding the sheep, the sheepherders, and the sheep-dogs that belonged to another sheep culture, the Anglo-American often failed.

Yet the historian Randall in his treatise on Sheep Husbandry in the United States probably expresses the consensus of opinion in praising the *pastor* dog by quoting two experienced men, one of his authorities, George W. Kendall, being as well known in the history of the sheep industry of Texas as he is in general for his *Narrative of the Texan Santa Fé Expedition.*[1]

After the pups are weaned, they never leave the particular drove among which they have been reared. Not even the voice of their master can entice them beyond sight of the flock; neither hunger nor thirst can do it. I have been credibly informed of an instance where a single dog having charge of a small flock of sheep was allowed to wander with them about the mountains, while the shepherd returned to his village for a few days, having perfect confidence in the ability of his dog to look after the flock during his absence, but with a strange want of foresight as to the provision of the dog for his food. Upon his return to the flock, he found it several miles from where he left it . . . and the poor, faithful dog in the agonies of death, dying of starvation, even in the midst of plenty; yet the flock had not been harmed by him. . . . The poor dog recognized the sheep only as brothers and dearly loved friends; he was ready at all times to lay down his life for them; to attack not only wolves and mountain-cats, with the confidence of victory, but even the bear, when there could be no hope. Of late years, when the shepherds of New Mexico have suffered so much from Indian marauders, instances have frequently occurred where the dog has not hesitated to attack his human foes, and although transfixed with arrows, his indomitable courage and faithfulness have

---

[1]Randall, Henry S., *Sheep Husbandry*, New York, 1860, pp. 284-286.

been such as to compel his assailants to pin him to the earth
with spears, and hold him there until dispatched with stones. . . .

These Mexican shepherds are very nomadic in character. They
are constantly moving about, their camp equipage consisting
merely of a kettle and a bag of meal; their lodges are made
in a few minutes, of branches, etc., thrown against cross-sticks.
They very seldom go out in the daytime with their flocks,
intrusting them entirely with their dogs, which faithfully return
them at night, never permitting any stragglers behind or lost.
Sometimes different flocks are brought into the same neighborhood owing to scarcity of grass, when the wonderful instincts
of the shepherds' dogs are most beautifully displayed; and to
my astonishment, who have been an eye-witness of such scenes,
if two flocks approach within a few yards of each other, their
respective proprietors will place themselves in the space between
them, and as is very naturally the case, if any adventurous
sheep should endeavor to cross over to visit her neighbors, her
dog protector kindly but firmly leads her back, and it sometimes happens, if many make a rush and succeed in joining
the other flock, the dogs under whose charge they are, go over
and bring them all out, but, strange to say, under such circumstances, they are never opposed by the other dogs. They approach
the strange sheep only to prevent their own family from leaving the flock, though they offer no assistance in expelling the
other sheep. But they never permit sheep not under canine
protection, nor dogs not in charge of sheep, to approach them.
Even the same dogs which are so freely permitted to enter
their flocks in search of their own are driven away with ignominy
if they presume to approach them without that laudable object
in view.

Many anecdotes could be related of the wonderful instinct
of these dogs. I have much doubt if there are shepherd dogs in
any other part of the world except Spain equal to those of
New Mexico in value. The famed Scotch and English dogs
sink into insignificance by the side of them. Their superiority
may be owing to the peculiar mode of rearing them, but they

113

are certainly very noble animals, naturally of large size, and highly deserving to be introduced into the United States. A pair of them will easily kill a wolf, and flocks under their care need not fear any common enemy to be found in our country.

—J. H. LYMAN.

Mr. Kendall speaks of meeting, on the Grand Prairie, "a flock numbering seventeen thousand, which immense herd was guarded by a very few men, assisted by a large number of noble dogs, which appeared gifted with the faculty of keeping them together. There was no running about, no barking or biting in their system of tactics; on the contrary, they were continually walking up and down, like faithful sentinels, on the outer side of the flock, and should any sheep chance to stray from its fellows, the dog on duty at that particular post, would walk gently up, take him carefully by the ear, and lead him back to the flock. Not the least fear did the sheep manifest at the approach of these dogs, and there was no occasion for it."

V. THE LOBO WOLF

When all the stories belonging to the drama of the sheep industry are collected, it will be found that while the element of tragedy appears oftenest in the sheepman's experience with the killing blizzard, the element of comedy is more likely to appear in his contacts with the coyote and the lone wolf. But it is a comedy of exasperation and frustration. In the lore of the Southwest's sheep range these two, akin though they be, are widely separate in the regard of the sheepman. Perhaps his own individualism made him respect the wolf, who always hunted alone. At any rate, the wolf story is invariably told with a certain amount of respect for that wily animal, while the coyote story is usually colored with vituperation. The coyote, though he is, as Mr. Gilfillan puts it, "the herder's nightmare and the sheepman's bogey," is a bogey that inspires the sheepman's contempt rather than

114

his fear. The wolf's meanness, on the other hand, had a quality that kept the sheepman forever intrigued.

The lobo wolf's partiality for sheep as prey and his uncanny concentration upon playing the role of villain of the sheep ranges make him, rather than the coyote, a folk character of importance in the sheep-raising business. There is not a community in the sheep-country without its own legend of one wily lobo wolf that forestalled capture for years. These stories are the white-stallion legends of the sheep range. Usually the wolf, after his first year of depredation, was given a name, a symbol of respect which man often pays to his animal contemporaries. The name was inevitably preceded by the adjective *old,* pronounced, of course, *ole.* A wolf that showed a certain peculiarity in his elusive track was dubbed *Old Three-Toes.* Another wolf villain in Bandera County that had had the temerity to show himself long before capture was named *Old Gray.* Still another wolf that won renown for his habit of hunting each night in pastures other than the ones in which his would-be capturers had planned to look for him, and then reversing his itinerary the next night, always managing to be where his hunters were not, was named *Old Smelder,* after a local legendary stock thief who had used the same tactics.

In the later days of the range, when sheepmen began to form into sheep-raising communities, and one lone wolf could become the common enemy of all, the wolf-hunt became a perennial event of importance and excitement. Staged at night, with one or many of the most noted of the community's packs of strong, lean wolf-hounds, and with the hunters on horseback and divided into groups, the hunt was an all-night affair in which sheepmen rode to hounds without benefit of red coats, and with an objective that was starkly utilitarian.

At these gatherings, at some period between dusk and dawn, there was always a chance for large relating of other

115

wolf hunts and other lobo wolves. The prestige of the wolf bandit in the story depended on how many thousands of dollars' damage he could amass to his credit while he defied all the powers of man to capture him. The man who finally effected the villain's capture, whether by running him to bay, or by trapping him, was always the hero of the piece, the St. George of the sheep range. In fact, so devastating is the lone wolf, and so difficult is his capture, that every sheepman secretly suspects that the ancient legend of the dragon-who-laid-waste-the-countryside had its true origin in some lobo wolf that preyed upon the sheep walks of antiquity.

VI. THE SHEARING CREW

Sheep-shearing time is a festival by tradition. In England the day after "t' clippin'" was given to sports by unwritten law. In the early Southwest, despite the fact that here the shearing was done by professional shearers roving like nomads from one sheep ranch to another, sheep-shearing was a social institution because it brought all the workers with sheep together. The herders, the rustler, and the shearing crew constituted a gathering wherein there was a great deal of talk and gossip and joking.

In some places shearing contests were held. This was an activity akin to the bronco-busting and calf-roping of the cowboy's rodeo. But the contestants were, too often, guilty of wounding the sheep in their unmerciful hurry to finish with him, and the practice as a competitive sport was discontinued.

In the early days the shearing crews were generally got together by a Mexican who called himself *capitán*. His crew consisted of from twenty-five to forty of the best shearers he could find, a cook, wool packers, and a boy who carried a can of worm medicine and a small brush to daub it with.

116

At the cry of "Coalie" or "Colero," he came to daub his medicine on such wounds as were made by the shearers, and there were usually plenty of them. There was also a *llanero,* who gathered up the fleeces as they came from the sheep, carrying each in an apron attached to his waist, to the packers, who in turn placed them in the seven-foot bags, packed them down, and sewed up the filled bags. Sometimes there was a sort of sub-boss who handed out checks to each shearer as he finished a sheep. He was expected to inspect the sheep as it was turned loose, and if the shearing had not been done effectively, he was to make the shearer catch the sheep again and remedy the defects. The *capitán* generally filled this post himself, as he was eager to have the shearing well done, and thus insure himself future employment from his patrons. The checks used were usually bits of tin cut from old cans and stamped in some way readily recognized by the *capitán.* These checks were legal tender in that particular sheep camp as long as the camp was maintained, and were used by the men in gambling among themselves or in payment of local purchases. The *capitán* redeemed them at a price agreed upon with his men.

Perhaps the most interesting individual in the shearing crew was the *capitán* himself. Always a man of some executive ability, and usually glorying in his high position, he was seldom imposed upon by his white patron. The foreman or rustler in charge seldom cared to argue overheatedly with thirty or forty Mexicans brandishing shears.

These are the folk characters belonging to the trail of the Golden Hoof. The tales they created belong to another chapter — a chapter which, let us hope, will someday be written, for, whether the stories are told in fact or in fiction, their worth to the Southwest's literature will be two-fold. First, they have definite story value in their own right because they project human beings against a peculiar and important environmental background; and, second, they are the stories of the growth of one of the two great industries of the West taken over by the Anglo-American when he took the land upon which they grew. As such, their lore and event and color must become an integral part of any collection of literature that seeks to record and preserve the flavor of the Southwest.

THE GHOST SHEEP DOG

By MERRILL BISHOP

"INSTINCT and training—what's the difference? Instinct in an animal needs no training. You can train some dogs to be good shepherds, but the best shepherd dog I ever heard anything about had absolutely nothing to do with men and men had absolutely nothing to do with him. Instinct is what comes into a creature either through ancestral blood or through food. They say, you know—these *pastor* people—that the milk any female gives any suckling carries the instincts of her kind."

I nodded. The man seemed to be a philosopher and not a mere watcher of sheep. His features and tones of voice expressed an incredulity not conveyed in the printed word. He went on.

"They—these Mexican sheep-herder people—used to tell about a dog over in the country between Devil's River and the Conchos that managed a flock of ghost sheep, grazing them on the prairie at night and bedding them by day in the breaks. He knew how to protect them against bad weather. He was a little black-and-white dog, not of the shepherd strain at all, a little dog scarcely bigger than a large gopher, a little gopher-built dog that seemed to run on his belly. Various *pastores* got a fleeting glimpse of him in moonlight, though no one ever laid hand on him. Nobody could see his sheep, however.

"Like the extraordinary offspring of some of the gods in old tales, this extraordinary dog, so the story went, was born out in the fields. No sooner was he born than his mother left him, frightened away by something strange, maybe a dog-repelling man, something. Anyhow, the puppy, its eyes still closed, was left to fare alone. Understand now, I am just telling you the story—not what I know."

The shepherd philosopher looked for encouragement; then he went on, while my thoughts turned for the moment to these English herders of olden days said to be dreamers very different from hilarious cow hands.

"It so happened that an old solitary ewe came along smelling the ground. Catching the dog scent, she naturally bristled up a bit as ewes will do. Then, seeing the pup did not move, she nosed it to investigate. Then the pup did the smelling. He was hungry. He had never suckled his own mother, but instinct guided him to the ewe's udder. I don't know where her lambs were. That makes no difference. She had milk.

"She responded to the sucking and lay down. Soon she got up, expecting that the lamb she had found would get up also, but it didn't. It just lay there and whimpered. Not knowing what else to do now, the ewe pushed it into some grass and hid it as she must have hidden many a lamb of her own. She grazed a little and then she came back and lay down by the pup and fed it. Night came, and she and the pup stayed together. The attachment between sheep and dog had begun. In the end she brought up the pup.

"Before a year had passed, the *pastor* people knew that a strange pup was wandering through the herds. The next thing they knew, this maturing pup, which was never to get big, was cutting out whatever sheep he wanted. Nobody saw him cutting out sheep, but the most careful and reliable *pastores* were losing sheep from their flocks. At the same time not a shepherd dog, not even the best trained and dependable dog, would attack the thief any more than a man would attack a ghost.

"The ghost dog, which wasn't exactly a ghost either, could be glimpsed occasionally, but, as I have said, the sheep he kept couldn't be seen. The *pastor* people decided that the ewe-

120

dog had changed the nature of his sheep so that they would feed at night like deer and stay asleep in some hidden place during the day. The ewe-dog had his flock established. That fact could not be doubted. Through the milk that had nurtured him the dog had an instinct that made him know the needs of his sheep; at the same time his proper blood made him a guard against coyotes.

"But no matter how many instincts there are, whether real or ghostly, it is the primal instinct that has always made the smartest of men and animals step aside. So the *pastor* people decided to use a female of his species to catch the dog that was stealing their sheep and turning them into ghosts. They had a bitch in heat and they put her out in a glade which, signs told them, the ghost herd was using. They told her to stay there. She obeyed.

"She stayed until the ewe-dog came along. The men who set the trap forgot that she might be as interested in the male as the male was in her. She followed him. In time she came back—alone. The ewe-dog about the same time quit stealing more sheep for his herd, though whether he quit guiding his ghost flock is not known.

"The female shepherd dog came back and had her litter of pups. They grew up squatty, with that gopher-like build, black-and-white. They became the most remarkable sheep dogs the country had ever known. Their sire transmitted into them the combined sheep and dog instincts that made him the master herder. To this day a man with a sheep dog to sell can get more for it, maybe, if he alleges that it descended from the ewe-dog.

"Men are worse than animals in lots of ways. They believe what they want to believe."

THE *PASTOR* AND THE SERPENT

By DAN STORM

OLD JESÚS MIRAVAL was an old-time Spanish-American sheep-herder, and walking had always been more than easy for him until the last couple of his eighty years. Yesterday I had told him that I would come to his house down the river if the weather was bad; at the same time he had promised me that he would come up to my house if the day turned out pretty. Now the air had that clean brightness that comes after a night of thunder-showering, and the piñon birds were flying in their little robber bands, turning as one bird and flashing their dark blue coats in the sun, racing the low, fast-flying clouds, and sending their roguish call of happiness to the tops of the hills. The whole world was bright with enchantment, and every creature, rock and blade of grass seemed to be listening to the songs inherent in the clean air, in the trees and on the waving grass. The wild hollyhocks and gilia and bluebells shone out brighter than ever before in their soft white, exciting red, and tender blue. On such a day as this rare thoughts are in the heart, and the feeling is everywhere that God has touched the world with one ray of the radiance of His land beyond the stars.

If this day couldn't bring Jesús, I would like to see the day that he called pretty, I was thinking, when, sure enough, here he came around the turn in the road by the pine tree, carrying something in his hand that might have been a cane. Then I remembered that he had told me of a surprise he had for me on this day, if God would do him the favor.

True to the general tone of the day, the old *pastor* walked

Dickens

lighter and not quite so stooped and appeared generally younger and more awake than on other days. Twenty steps from me he began to smile and hold up a small stick about a yard long.

"Buenos días, Danielito," he called in his melodious voice. "How do you like the day given to us by our God?" I told him that I was glad the day was good because it brought me my good friend to spend the pretty hours with me.

Straightway I began to notice that the stick he carried was a last year's yucca stalk. A gut string was tied to one end; into the other end a key, made also of yucca and modeled after a violin peg, was inserted. Around this peg was wound the other end of the gut string. At first I thought it was a bow for shooting arrows, but then I knew it must be some kind of musical instrument, although I could not imagine how one would go about playing it. It was clearly a kind of one-string violin, or guitar, or shepherd's harp.

When I asked the old man what this thing was, he said that it was *una música* (a music, or a music maker). *"Es música de pastor, música borregero,"* he said. (It is a music of the shepherd, sheepherder's music.) "A music not very loud, but what does a man need with loud music when he is by himself with only his sheep for company, and only the coyotes talking at night, and no one to listen to his music but his own self and the hills—the hills."

While he talked, he tightened the peg of his shepherd's harp and put the stalk against one corner of his mouth. Adjusting his mustache, he began, changing the size of his mouth for his notes and plucking the single string, something in the manner of one playing a Jew's harp. The music was faint and fairy-like. The first piece he played was something like an old Spanish polka, something like "Turkey in the Straw," "The Campbells Are Coming," and "Buffalo Gals," all rolled into one. That was the main piece for him, though he played

123

others, and this *pastor* was the first man I ever saw and heard play on this instrument. It was strange enough to see such a wild and rustic harp played in so weird and ingenious a manner; but it was far more surprising that the music coming out of it at the mastery of this weather- and time-beaten old shepherd would be so transcendent.

There was never any music like this. It was soft and faint, and the more delicate strains were like organ tones coming on the wind from elfland, the land of all the childhood dreams, the land of the deepest hopes of human hearts. Whispered, yet clear, came the echoes of fairy flutes. Like music first breaking in upon a summer dream, it made the heart hold its breath for fear of waking and finding the music gone.

The voice of the little harp came, returning something which you thought forgotten but which had not forgotten you. Someone long sought and longed for in some other incarnation called faintly to you in this little music and said that at last what you wanted most you should yet have. The fears and regrets of life came faintly knocking and were wafted away in a whirling, laughing dance. Then the heart choked with ecstacy and begged for the strains not to stop. All the lullabies and songs of waterfalls and windy pines and the cries of all beloved birds were in this magic music.

As old Jesús played on his *música,* he awakened a spark of things not perceived by mortal senses. Time and again have I tried to play the harp as he played it, but though the music has been sweet to my ears, it has never been what old Jesús made.

He was a great hand to tell stories that he had lived or seen —or, perhaps dreamed—no telling where. There was something in the telling of them that took you into his world. And now, on this fine day, after he had played on the yucca fiddle for a correct while and then presented it to me, and after we had eaten, flavoring our *frijoles* with a little of the cider that

124

the Rio Ruidoso of New Mexico provides, Jesús the sheepherder told me some of the stories he knew I liked so well to
hear.

Night and day for sixty years with my sheep. Would I not
in those years have seen things others might think impossible?
There used to be creatures in this world that do not exist now
except in regions little visited by men. In these hills used to
live serpents who were more wise than men, and they had
powers very magical and terrible.

Listen! One day when I was drifting my sheep to the top
of a hill, playing on my *música*, I heard a strong wind coming from the crest. It came like the wind coming down the
chimney in winter. *Shuuuuu,* like that. But this was a strange
wind. It was in one stream and nowhere else, like a thin
current of water. And it was not blowing me from behind as
ordinary winds do, or pushing against me, but was pulling
me forward, like a great sucking breath. I tried to throw
myself backwards, but my forces left me. I was powerless in
this wind, and was being steadily pulled toward the top of
the hill, straight toward a white post taller than a man, thicker
than a man's thigh.

Imagine my fear when I saw that this was not a post but a
serpent many times bigger than a rattlesnake and very ugly.
And with its devil breath it was sucking me steadily towards
it, little by little. What remedy? Closer he drew me and
louder became the noise of his breath. I could see his eyes:
now green, now red, now blue. In my terror I thought of my
godfather, Mariano, a man very religious and wise. I am
Catholic and at times like this more so than ever. So I crossed
myself. Immediately I remembered that godfather Mariano
had told me these serpents are helpless against things of the
Holy Faith. I could almost touch the animal now, and could

see his white body growing smaller and larger as he drew his breath in and let it out.

Summoning all my forces, I quickly drew a cross with my finger in the air right in front of his face. His breath stopped and I stood still. The serpent, very terrified, uncoiled and went down the hill with an expression of great fear on its face.

That is the last I have seen of that serpent. But remember: the way to defend yourself against his kind is to make the sign of the cross in front of him. Then the evil wind will stop. If you do not believe what I have told you, I will prove everything. I will take you to the very hill where this serpent stood.

Yes, this story ends happily. But it is long. You will not fall asleep, Danielito? Then I need a little tobacco while I tell this *historia*. What matters the length of the story if it ends well? Ready. Watch out. Pay good attention.

Bueno. This was a shepherd very, very poor. When he was twenty years old his father turned him loose in the world to seek his life. This *pastor* had with him four dogs as astute and fore-telling as people. His dogs did everything: watched the sheep, drove off the *tigres*, wildcats, wolves, and all the other fierce animals. Every day the dogs would count the sheep and look for the ones missing.

It was one day after a long time of drouth that the *pastor* was journeying through the land treading on grass that was very sad, when he came to the banks of a river. Here he spread his blanket and made camp. The next morning his dogs awoke him very early and told him that the river was very angry, that rain had come in the mountains filling the river with water so abundant the banks could hardly contain it. Arising, the *pastor* beheld the river black and foaming, roaring in wrath, and carrying on its back great logs and

126

drifts, which bounded and leaped against each other, smiting the banks—a sight terrible to see.

"Now yes," said the *pastor*, "I will have much wood." Saying this, he sent one of his dogs to fetch his rope, and the dog came coiling the rope in his mouth, and gave it to the *pastor,* who stood on the bank where the river made a turn. Without delay the *pastor* began throwing his rope upon the logs and sticks floating down the river, pulling them ashore and piling them into a heap to dry.

A huge log very fat came riding down the river and the *pastor* roped it, calling to his dogs to help him drag it in when he found himself being pulled into the river. The dogs took hold with their mouths and the log began to come toward the bank. When they had almost landed the log, the *pastor* noticed that there was something on it. It was a serpent large and pure white. And he was crying and crying and calling out from time to time the name of some girl.

The language of these serpents is almost like Spanish; so the *pastor* spoke to this one.

"My friend," he said, "why are you throwing tears into the already swollen river?"

"Ahi," said the serpent, "I have been four days floating down the river on this log, unable to get off. I am following my daughter, who was lost when the river came up. Have you not seen her come by here on one of these logs? Oh, I must find my poor Amanda. Where could she be?"

"Then," said the *pastor*, "how much will you give me if I help you find your daughter?"

"The *pastor* did not really want anything, but he wanted to see what the serpent would say.

The serpent became very much excited and said to the *pastor*, "If you help me find my daughter, I will give you a power that will be worth more to you than gold."

"What power is that?" asked the *pastor*.

127

"It is something great," said the serpent.

"But what?" said the *pastor*.

"Help me and you shall see," said the serpent.

So the *pastor* held a conference with his dogs, and one of them said it had seen the daughter go down the river earlier in the morning. And another said he had seen the log hit the bank down the river and watched the daughter climb onto the bank.

So the *pastor* pointed down the river and said, "Down there somewhere is your daughter. This dog will show you where."

Then the serpent, very happy, went leaping down the river, following the dog, shouting, "Amanda! Amanda!"

Soon the daughter heard the cries of her father and came running and both were happy.

Very glad, the serpent came back to the *pastor* and said, "Now I will give you what I promised." So saying, he wound himself about the *pastor* and kissed him four times on the cheek, and said, "Now you can understand the language of all the creatures in the world. But if you ever say anything that you have heard them say, whether fish, animals of claw or hoof, or creatures with wings or any other kind of animal, you will die."

So the *pastor* and the serpent said *"Adios"* and went their roads. More rains fell and the grass in all the land was happy and all the birds were laughing. The *pastor* was very contented; so he went home and cooked one of his father's beeves for a celebration for himself and his dogs. While he was preparing the animal, there came circling from afar in the sky many crows. Perching in trees near by, they fell to talking, and the *pastor* heard them say they had not eaten anything for days. So he and the dogs sat in a circle about the fire at their dinner and the dogs sat up eating with good manners. After they were through, the *pastor* threw much of the meat to the crows, who ceased their talking and began eating rapidly.

Their hunger satisfied and their hearts glad, the crows began talking all at once about a great treasure hidden in the ground: five trunks all holding a burro load each. Long had they searched and not until now had they found a man good enough of heart to deserve the treasure. It would be well if this *pastor* should find it. There was a golden key, they said, hidden in the hollow of an oak tree at the head of a canyon not far away. The crows talked so fast that the *pastor* could hardly understand what they were saying, but he listened with the ears of a coyote and missed nothing.

Soon the crows flew chattering away from their trees, and when they had disappeared up the river and over the hills, the *pastor* leaped up and called his dogs. The dogs became excited and ran about in circles, barking and leaping. But the *pastor* bade them be silent lest they arouse whoever might be about.

After much searching, the *pastor* found the key wrapped in a map in the hollow of an old oak tree on the hill. Following with beating heart the directions of the map, he came to an old, old mine almost caved in and full of many spider webs. Entering the tunnel, he found a door fastened with a huge lock. Into the lock he thrust the key with trembling hand. In an instant there echoed through the cave a great noise of old hinges squeaking. Dirt and rocks scattered everywhere as five lids opened on five trunks, showing each to be full of gold coins that shone so brightly as to light up the far corners of the vast cave.

No shadow was left in the old mine, so bright was the gold. Like a man distracted, the *pastor* went leaping from one trunk to the other saying, *"Válgame Dios!* What fortune is mine! It is not true! It cannot be true!"

And he would take handfuls of the coins and let them

129

slip through his fingers. He kept saying, "Gold! Gold! Gold! It is not possible!" Then he became terribly frightened, thinking that he had gone crazy. Then he felt his reason actually leaving him. He began filling his pockets till he could hardly walk, and then he started to run out of the cave; but he could not, so tired he was. So he fell over beside the cave and lay there breathing hard with the sweat running off his forehead. Thus he lay until he had rested and recovered his senses.

Next day the *pastor* came with five burros and loaded all the trunks of gold upon them. First he went to see his father, to whom he gave one burro load.

"Father," said the *pastor*, "I have hunted my life in the world and now that I have this money, I believe I would like to visit the *plazas* of the world, and travel."

So the father said that this was all right.

Bueno. The pastor went from plaza to plaza throughout all the country. First through the rich part of a city he paraded with his burros laden with shining gold so that all might see a sight so rare. Then into the part of town he would go where the poor lived. And at every poor house he would leave some gold—a hundred pesos here, five hundred pesos there, and here a thousand. All throughout the land people were saying that here was the first rich man they had ever seen who would reach his hand into his pocket for the poor. Not just half his hand did he put into his pocket but all of his hand up to his elbow. Always with him were his four dogs, and he always remembered that the serpent had told him about never telling a thing he had heard the animals say.

The time came when the *pastor* thought about getting a wife. He went to one of the poor homes he had visited and married a young woman. Now he thought he was doing a noble thing to marry this poor girl; and the girl thought herself very fortunate to be the wife of this man so good and so rich. But as time went on, she began to ask him many questions about how he got all his wealth. But the *pastor* would avoid answering her, and would never tell, though it seemed to him at times he must tell or his wife's questions would drive him crazy.

One day, with his secret gift of understanding the language of the animals beating in his brain, he went again to the old mine to see if he could find any more treasure. He opened the same lock that had opened all the five trunks, and when the door opened, there were five more trunks. The lids flew open and out of each trunk sprang the heads of hundreds of serpents. The *pastor* shrank back in fear, pale and trembling. He knew that this was a warning that he must never tell anything he heard the animals say.

After the *pastor* had been married for some months, he and his wife took a journey into the mountains. On the way, he was listening to the horses they were riding. The horses were talking, and suddenly, forgetting himself, he began to smile at the conversation of the horses, and then, not thinking of the unfortunate thing he had done, laughed out loud.

His wife looked at him closely and then said very sharply, "What are you laughing at?"

The *pastor* started as he realized his bad move and sat upon his horse silent for several moments with his tongue jumping about in his mouth hunting for words.

"Oh," he said finally, "I was only laughing at the way very funny in which the beasts were neighing. What a strange sound it is, for the truth; I had not noticed it till just now."

"Aha," said the wife, "you are not fooling me. I know that you can understand what they say. You are a *brujo* (witch). They are talking about me, and you are laughing. Tell me what they are saying."

Now the horses probably were not saying anything funny

131

at all. But it seemed funny to man's ears; that is all. They could have been talking about grass soup, loco weed whiskey, or alfalfa tortillas or such a simple thing as that.

"My dear," said the *pastor*, "I am just feeling happy today. Anything makes me laugh. I laugh very easily anyhow. See how that whirlwind in the sand makes me smile already. Ha, ha, ha! Ho, ho, ho! How funny it is." And the *pastor* nearly fell from his horse with laughing.

"Tell me, I say," said the wife, very serious.

"Yes, yes," the *pastor* went on, "I laugh at anything. Now you see that tree over there. The wind is blowing it in such a way that it makes me think of a fat man very drunk. Ha, ha, ha! how funny it—"

But his wife would not let him finish. She screamed this time and said, "Tell me what the horses are saying or I will not go another step," and she reined her horse to a stop.

"All right," said the *pastor*; "go to the store and buy me two-bits' worth of nails, two-bits' worth of boards, two-bits' worth of hammers, so that I can make myself a box. Because when I tell you what you ask, I will fall dead."

And the wife, very anxious to hear what the horses were saying, beat her horse two steps to each jump to the store and met the *pastor* at their house with all the two-bits' worth of things.

"Now," said the *pastor*, "listen closely to what I am going to tell you. Do you see this beautiful pistol?"

And the pastor aimed at his wife and fired. Loud noise and smoke filled the room and the wife fell down and died, well killed—think you not so, Danielito? Long was the story but it is short now because it is ended, and what matter if the story took much time if it ended well?

Ah! you say the story ends sad. How can it be sad if a shameless and cruel woman receives the punishment she

132

well deserves? You had rather have the good kind *pastor* die? Ah, what a Danielito you are! You think that a sad story is happy. I do not understand you.

More tobacco. Thank you, Danielito. This work I am going to do for you making your house very pretty soon, I will begin. Thanks for the *dos reales,* my boy.

Ah, Daniel, I must tell you. Do not feel badly. The story was not as I have told it. The truth is that, just when the *pastor* was about to go back to his house and meet his wife, his four dogs began looking very anxiously in the air and called the *pastor's* attention to a great band of crows flying toward him. The crows came and told him that he could tell his wife his secret if he wanted to because he had been just and generous with his wealth. The *pastor* meant really to make his own death, so good and unselfish he was. But the wife came without the two-bits' worth of things and said she did not want the *pastor* to die. Then the *pastor* told her everything. This is the true story, and I told you the other to see if you have a good heart. *Gracias* for the tobacco, Danielito.

A MEXICAN FOLK VERSION
OF KING MIDAS

By W. A. WHATLEY

THE following version of the myth of King Midas and the
Ass's Ears was told me by Celso Domingues, a Mexican
cowboy of Baqueteros in the State of Chihuahua, Mexico.
Celso and all his connections gave every evidence, so far as
I could see, of having been virgin to the alphabet for gen-
erations, and it is highly doubtful that he came by the tale
from any direct literary source.

"There was once a long time ago a king in a very far
away country who was afflicted by God with a most humili-
ating deformation. Horns grew upon his head—a fine pair
of sheep's horns, curling up close to his head just over and
behind his ears. This king suffered great humiliation because
of the horns, which he, however, contrived to keep secret
from his subjects by brushing his hair over them, for he
knew that if his people once learned that their king had a
pair of sheep's horns on his head they would lose all respect
for him and his authority, and his name would become a
by-word.

"All went as well as could be expected for a while, and
the king kept on frizzling his hair up over the horns in
secret, but with the passing of time his hair grew so long
that he began to look shaggy, and his servants began to
wonder and even to pass remarks. The king realized that
he would soon have to have his hair trimmed, so he called
in his barber and told him privately of his misfortune,
showed him the disgraceful horns, and promised him great

134

rewards if he kept the secret, and also instant death if he told the matter to anyone. The barber promised, and the king appeared next day with neatly trimmed hair.

"But the barber was as garrulous as are all those of his trade, and the possession of such a piece of gossip without being able to share it with anyone preyed upon him until he was nigh unto death. He did not dare impart his knowledge of the scandalous matter, for fear of his life; yet the silence imposed upon him was such an agony that he felt he would go mad if he did not find some relief.

"At last, after a sleepless night, he hit upon a plan. Rising at dawn, he went to a solitary field in the outskirts and dug a large hole, into which he thrust his head. Thus, headforemost in the hole with his voice muffled by the earth, he shouted repeatedly until the load on his soul was lightened, 'King Fulano has horns! King Fulano has horns!'[1]

"Having thus relieved his mind of the tormenting secret, he returned home and lived in peace, and the matter no longer troubled him; and all went well until the rainy season. But when the rains came and the grass sprouted, a strange plant grew up from the hole into which the barber had shouted the fatal secret, and when the curious came near to examine it, they found inscribed in large letters on its broad leaves the words, 'King Fulano has horns!' "

* * * * *

The essentials of the original Greek version are as follows: King Midas, for spiting the gods, was afflicted with ass's ears, which he contrived to hide under his hair. Fearing to trust a barber with his secret, he required of his wife that she trim and dress his hair, at the same time enjoining her silence on the matter under heavy penalties. But she, being

---

[1]*"El rey Fulano tiene cuernos!"*—Fulano is roughly equivalent to "John Doe" or "So-and-So."

135

a talkative woman, fond of gossip, found the secret too much for her to contain entirely, and at last, in her extremity, she went privately down to the delta where the river flows into the sea, and whispered softly to the rushes on the banks, "King Midas has ass's ears! King Midas has ass's ears!"

But ever after, when the breeze blew over the water and stirred the rushes, they would rustle and whisper together, and utter audibly, "King Midas has ass's ears! King Midas has ass's ears!"

TORTILLA MAKING

By RUTH DODSON

IT HAS NOT been so many years since the metate was the one indispensable article of furniture in the home of the Texas-Mexican. If a young couple, starting housekeeping, did not possess an heirloom in the form of a well-worn metate, a new one could be bought for ten dollars. But a metate there had to be, or there would be no bread—no tortillas.

Even now, during lean years, or times of the year when there is little money with which to buy flour, it is necessary to revert to the cheaper tortilla. Since women of the present generation find the use of the metate too slow and too strenuous for them to learn the art of using it, a handmill makeshifts for the metate—and the quality of the tortilla suffers thereby. But there are still Mexicans of an older generation who do not begrudge the work nor the time spent at grinding corn on a metate in order to have good tortillas. This work belongs to them; it is a part of their heritage.

The metate—the grinding stone, with its *mano*—the four-sided stone pestle, that is as long as the metate is wide—is too well known, if only in pictures, to make a description necessary. But the actual use of this tool, and the method of making tortillas, is, usually, only vaguely known by even those who eat tortillas. The process of making them is slow and long.

Suppose that the Mexican cook is to make tortillas. She takes some corn—and let it be remembered that corn swells when cooked—and puts it into a cooking vessel—an iron pot, an olla, or, perhaps, a little battered brass kettle—whatever

137

is available. A small quantity of lime, say a half-cupful, is put into a tin, likely an empty tomato can. This is placed in the vessel on top of the corn, and water is poured into it, overflowing onto the corn, which the lime water turns yellow. Experience tells, by the color of the corn, when enough lime water has been used. The gritty sediment of the lime remains in the can, which is taken out and set aside. A generous amount of water is added to the pot and it is put on a slow fire to simmer.

After the corn has cooked sufficiently, the husk will slip when a grain is rubbed between thumb and finger. It can also be tested by biting a grain; if the teeth break the grain with only a small amount of resistance, it is cooked enough. If it should be cooked too much, the dough will be sticky; if not cooked enough, the dough will be lacking in adhesiveness.

The corn, known at this stage as *nixtamal*, is allowed to become perfectly cold. When the cook is ready to grind it, she takes as much as she needs for one making of tortillas. This is washed through three waters while it is rubbed between the hands. The thick yellow lime water is thus removed and the corn, or *nixtamal*, remains clean and white.

The metate, which is usually kept in a leaning position against the wall, is placed right side up with the *mano*, the pestle, resting across the lower part of it. The cook then takes her place, on her knees, at the highest end of it. The first thing to be done is to wash both the metate and the *mano* clean of the dry *masa*, the dry dough, that was left on them from the last grinding. This *masa* has prevented dust from settling in the roughened surface of the stone, which would make it very difficult to clean.

The *nixtamal*, which is in a container and covered with clear water, is placed conveniently at the right side. A pan is placed under the lower end of the metate to catch the

138

masa as it is ground. The *mano,* when at rest, is always at the lower end of the metate.

A double handful of *nixtamal* is now dipped out of the water and placed at the upper end of the metate, in a little mound that trails off toward the *mano.* The *mano* is grasped near each end and drawn up toward the operator, who holds it firmly, but tilts it slightly. This crowds the *nixtamal* and catches some of it under the *mano,* where, with a firm pressure, it is crushed; then the *mano* is tilted in the opposite direction and the crushed *nixtamal,* which is coarse *masa* now, is pushed to the lower end of the metate, where it falls off into the pan. The *nixtamal* is replenished as needed, and there are pauses when it is sprinkled lightly with water, or shaped so that the *mano* can involve as much as possible— which at most is very little. These pauses serve as brief rest periods. For, while the *mano,* which weighs several pounds, is in operation, the body of the worker swings back and forth, and up and down, in a rhythmic and leisurely, but tiring, manner. The work is hard, and it is of a nature that does not invite hurry.

Now the *masa* is emptied onto the metate and shaped into a ball. This mass of coarse dough is placed at the upper part of the metate as the *nixtamal* was. The heel of the hand is pressed into it and a small portion is smeared down toward the lower part of the metate. The *mano* is turned to its smoothest side, which is usually that on the opposite side from that used in the breaking of the *nixtamal.* Then the *remoliendo,* the re-grinding, begins. The movement of the *mano* is similar to that of the first grinding, but smoother — and slower—making a *masa* of smooth, adhesive texture, which, when it reaches the end of the metate, falls into the pan in broad flakes. When all the *masa* is ground, it is made into a ball as before. Then it must be taken through the metate once again.

139

In this case the *mano* is carried up and down with more tilting, and each time the *masa* is carried only near to the edge of the metate, where the *mano* is tilted abruptly and then withdrawn, leaving a little ridge of *masa*. This is added to until there is enough for one tortilla. Then, with the hand turned palm upward, the *masa* is scooped up by drawing the hand from right to left along the edge of the metate. This leaves a shell-shaped mass in the hand that is known as a *testal*. The *testal* is laid lightly in the receptacle at the end of the metate. When all the *masa* is made into *testales*, the metate is leaned against the wall with the *mano* resting across it.

Now a smooth sheet of iron known as a *comal* is put near the fire on supporting rocks and a few coals of fire are raked under it. The typical *comal* is saucer-shaped—like the basin of the Comal River at New Braunfels, Texas. Coals will be added as needed to keep the *comal* at an even heat. The cook seats herself on the ground near the *comal* with the *testales* near at hand. There will also be a small receptacle with water in it, a basket with a cloth in it, and a small greasy rag. The cook dips her fingers into the water and rubs her hands together to moisten them. She then takes a *testal* between the palms of her hands and shapes it into a round flat cake—it will be about the size of an old-fashioned biscuit. Then it will be patted and gradually carried to the fingers, where it will be patted and turned at the same time until it is a tortilla of a size according to the skill of the maker. The eye will detect no difference in the sizes of tortillas of the entire batch. An expert might make them as large as a dinner plate and as thin as a wafer, but the usual size is about that of a breakfast plate. In Sonora and other parts of Mexico the tortilla is sometimes made as large as two feet in diameter.

When the tortilla reaches the size that is the standard of a

140

particular cook, she takes the greasy cloth and rubs it on the *comal*, and with the utmost skill lays the tortilla on it. While it is cooking she proceeds to pat out another one. When the tortilla cooks on one side, she dips the fingers of her right hand into the water, shakes the excess off, and lightly touches the tortilla, which sticks to her fingers slightly. She raises it off the *comal*, and, with a gentle flip, turns it over. All the while she is holding, clinging to her slightly turned left hand, a tortilla in whatever stage of making it happens to be. If the *comal* is large enough, it may have several tortillas on it at the same time in various stages of being cooked— and the patting is hardly interrupted by the attention to the tortillas on the *comal*. As they are cooked, they are placed in the basket and kept covered with the cloth.

The current price of tortillas, in at least one small Texas town, is a penny each—they used to be a dime a dozen. And they are made by way of the metate!

NAVAJO SKETCHES

By *YANH-NA-BAH*

THE WHIRLWIND

Two little boys were herding sheep on the desert. For miles one could see a moving object such as a man on horseback. The day was beautiful and calm. The sun shone bright.

"Come, Kee, I'll tell you a story," said Haskie.

Haskie was ten years old, and Kee was two years older than his brother.

"Let the sheep graze, and we will sit on top of this hill from where we can see everything around us," said Haskie.

Without saying a word, Kee walked slowly. At last he sat by his brother. "Now, what is it that you wish to tell me?" he asked as he looked across the desert. Then suddenly he added, "Look! Do you see that whirlwind?"

"Yes. Doesn't it look beautiful? It reaches up into the clouds. It looks like a long, slender cloud itself," answered Haskie.

"Beautiful? Why do you say it's beautiful? You must never say that again. If mother heard you she'd—oh, I don't know what she'd do to you."

"Why do you talk so? Whenever I say that a thing is beautiful, you always tell me that I must never say it," said Haskie.

"How about the story that you were going to tell me?" asked Kee.

"Instead of my telling you the story, suppose you tell me about the whirlwind," said Haskie.

142

There was not a breeze; yet the whirlwind was slowly going across the desert.

Kee thought that it was his duty to explain things to his brother. A few minutes passed without a word being said.

"You see, younger brother, there are 'chindi,' evil spirits, in the whirlwind. They do us harm, and we fear them. Anything that will harm us isn't beautiful. When a whirlwind comes near us, or when we are going to be caught in a whirlwind, we shout, 'Na da nih' (your son-in-law). If we say this, it will not approach us. It will only go in the opposite direction, just as a mother will not approach her son-in-law for fear she will go blind."

They sat on the hill and watched the whirlwind go across the desert. The sheep grazed calmly at the foot of the small hill on which they were sitting.

Haskie said, "I often wondered why people always shouted, 'Na da nih! Na da nih.' Now I know."

FLEEING FROM THE COYOTES

IT was dawn, and Kinibah was in the habit of getting up early. She put her blanket around her shoulders. It was her custom to pray to Mother Dawn. She walked away from the hogan and stopped. Taking some corn-pollen from her small bag, she prayed, "May the things that I do cause others to be happy." She put a pinch of corn-pollen on top of her head. "May I walk in happiness today," she prayed as she sprinkled some pollen toward the horizon. She turned and went back to the hogan. As she walked slowly toward it, she thought of the coyotes that had howled the night before.

Her daughter was still sleeping when she went back into the hogan.

"Habai, it is time for you to get up," said Kinibah as she pulled the blankets away from her daughter. "Here is the corn-pollen."

"Is it dawn already?" Habai asked.

"Yes."

Habai went out and prayed just as her mother had done. Her prayer was the same as her mother's. When she came back, her mother was cooking breakfast.

"Did you hear the coyotes howl last night?" asked Kinibah.

"Yes, I did," said Habai. "Do you suppose it means anything? You know I am almost afraid to tell you what I think it means."

"The night before last they came, too," said her mother as she went about preparing breakfast. "You've heard about these men who run around in coyotes' skins, haven't you? But there are people who don't believe it."

"Yes, I have," answered Habai. "Hatali Nez's two sons run around in coyotes' skins. They come to people's homes, especially people whom they wish to harm."

"At night they go into a deserted hogan and sing a special song. Then they put on the skin with the help of some spirit. They howl like coyotes," said the mother.

Kinibah believed in evil spirits. She had her own pagan religion. Habai wondered why they were eating breakfast early. Usually they fed the pet lambs and milked the goats before breakfast, but this morning they didn't.

"After breakfast, my child," said the mother, "we'll clean the hogan. I want to shake my hand, so as to find out what is the meaning of the coyotes' coming around our hogan." She was one who shook her hands in order to find out things that she wanted to know.

"Take out all the sheepskins and shake them," said the mother.

When everything was in order, Habai sat on a sheepskin by her mother. Her mother put corn-pollen on her fingers from the tip to the wrist. After doing this she closed her eyes and began to shake her hand. "Why did the coyotes come last

144

night?" she murmured. "Tell me. I want to know. I don't
know why they have come, now, for two nights." She repeated
these same sentences over and over. She paused for a minute.

"I see. Yes—we must move? We must move from our winter hogan?" Her hands shook more than ever.

Habai looked in silence. She knew what it meant.

"Immediately. Very soon," her mother murmured. Her
hands stopped shaking. She opened her eyes and prayed.

Habai watched her mother. She did not dare ask her any
questions.

"Dear child, we have to move to our summer home. We
can't stay here any longer. The coyotes that we have been
hearing will come again tonight. They really are men in
coyotes' skins. They want to poison us," said her mother.

"Did you find out who these men were?" asked Habai.

"Yes, but now we must pack up our things and flee with
our sheep. We must not spend another night in our winter
hogan," said the mother.

Habai packed up a few things which they would need at
their summer home. Her mother rushed here and there, putting things away in the hogan. Before long they were on their
way.

THE ROADRUNNER IN FACT AND FOLK-LORE

By J. FRANK DOBIE

BORN and reared in Southwest Texas, I was grown before I knew that the bird had any other name than paisano (pronounced pie-sah'-no), by which Mexicans of Texas and northern Mexico know it. The word means *fellow-countryman, compatriot, native.* It is sometimes said to be a corruption of *faisán* (pheasant), a word changed in some Mexican local-

ities to *faisano.* Yet the bird belongs to the cuckoo, and not to the pheasant, family. Its scientific name, *geococcyx californianus,* signifies "ground cuckoo," the type specimen having been collected in California. It is known to Mexicans also as *corre camino* (runs the road), *churella, churrea,* and other names.

The names in English are just as numerous, varying according to locality. Roadrunner, chaparral cock, chaparral bird, and chaparral are the more common names, exclusive of paisano—which name I intend to keep on using, because

146

it expresses a quality that is to me fundamental. The bird and I are fellow natives of the country. Lizard bird, war bird, snake-eater, medicine bird, cock of the desert, and ground cuckoo are names met with in print, though not used to any extent, I think, by people belonging to the land. I have never met "bird-of-paradise" as a name except in the well-worn anecdote of the West Texas real estate agent—this was before the "realtors" arrived—who in answer to his prospective client's question, "What's that bird?" replied, "Bird-of-paradise, some folks call it," whereupon the stranger commented, "He's a hell of a long ways from home, ain't he?"

In 1932 the Texas Folk-Lore Society adopted the paisano as its emblem. It is the State bird of New Mexico. Perhaps no other native bird of North America, excepting the eagle and the turkey, which the Aztecs had domesticated long before Columbus sailed, has been so closely associated with the native races of this continent. It appears in the mythology, songs and legends of more than one tribe of Indians. English-speaking men living over the paisano's range—Texas, New Mexico, Arizona, California, most of Mexico, and into Colorado, Oklahoma, and Kansas—have generated an interest in it that not even unjust persecution has diminished. Descriptions of the bird, with emphasis always on its long legs, a tail that serves as a brake, running ability, brilliantly colored head, comical antics and insectivorous appetite, are to be found in many books. But the best description I know is Eve Ganson's in her delightful and delightfully illustrated *Desert Mavericks*.

> The Road-Runner runs in the road,
> His coat is speckled, à la mode.
> His wings are short, his tail is long,
> He jerks it as he runs along.
> His bill is sharp, his eyes are keen,
> He has a brain tucked in his bean.

147

> But in his gizzard — if you please —
> Are lizards, rats, and bumble bees;
> Also horned toads — on them he feeds —
> And rattlesnakes! and centipedes!

The roadrunner is the most interesting bird of the Southwest.

I. FACTS

"On Them He Feeds"

Now that the urban hunter is envious of every quail that makes the morning cheerful and the evening tranquil with his call, the roadrunner has been charged with eating quail eggs and killing and eating young quail, and is even being killed out in many places on the assumption that this charge is true. It is a pity that authentic evidence is not as easy for the public to digest as superstition and rumor.

During the summer of 1938 Roy Bedichek, who is a good ornithologist, was on a United States Wild Life Refuge in southern Texas in company with a man employed by the government to help "balance nature." This man carried a gun and had, he said, "orders from Washington" to kill roadrunners off the refuge. "Why?" Bedichek asked. "Oh, because they eat other birds." Bedichek proposed to examine the craws of two roadrunners killed. The contents, spread out on white paper, consisted of nothing but legs and wings of grasshoppers—nothing else at all.

In the early spring of 1932 two paisanos killed in the country near San Antonio were brought to the Witte Museum, where Mrs. Ellen Schulz Quillin examined the crops. In the crop of one killed on a cool day were found twenty-one snails, one cutworm, one bee, one spider, three daddy-longlegs, two pods of a nettle, two crickets, seven small beetles, two June bugs. In the crop of the other, killed on a warm

148

day, were found thirty-one cutworms, twelve snails, nine beetles, one cricket, and many moths.

In *Arizona Wild Life,* October, 1932, D. M. Gorsuch of the U. S. Biological Survey printed a very interesting report on the food habits of roadrunners as determined by field observation and the official examination of one hundred road-runners taken in close proximity to quail at a time when the quail were nesting or were leading their broods afield. Grass-hoppers constituted 62 per cent of the stomach contents of the hundred roadrunners examined. Other insects included centipedes, scorpions, and tarantulas. The reptilian contents were mostly lizards, but part of a rattlesnake was found. "No evidence of quail or their eggs was found," although two cactus wrens, an unidentified sparrow, and a nestling meadow lark were found.

"About two years ago," Mr. Gorsuch continues, "I saw a roadrunner following a family of twelve newly hatched Gambel quail and their parents, as they fed through the grass. This appeared to be a splendid opportunity for the roadrunner to secure one of the chicks, for although the adult quail knew of its presence, they gave it little attention. The roadrunner's interest centered upon those grasshoppers that the quail started up and that flew beyond their reach. This continued until the roadrunner darted immediately in front of the cock quail to get a grasshopper, whereupon the cock turned and savagely attacked the roadrunner, who escaped by jumping into a mesquite, from which it sailed into an adjoining wash. On many other occasions a like proceeding has been observed, and it is my conviction that the roadrunner follows such feeding quail for the grass-hoppers thus started up."

Just so, roadrunners—like robins and blackbirds—some-times follow a plow to get the worms exposed. The procedure is common in wild life. I have seen cowbirds hanging around the heads of grazing cattle to catch the insects routed out by the grazers. Gulls, terns, and other shore birds follow boats to catch the mullet dispersed. Coyotes squat around badgers to catch the rats that the badgers chase out of nests they are digging into. During the drouth of 1935 in Southwest Texas, while ranchers around Brady were singeing off spines from prickly pear so that their stock could eat it, two men reported to a friend of mine that roadrunners followed the pear-burner every day searching the singed pear for roasted worms and bugs.

In 1916 the University of California issued a pamphlet on *Habits and Food of the Roadrunner in California,* by Harold C. Bryant. Insects comprised 74.93 per cent of the contents of the stomachs of eighty-four roadrunners examined. No quail were found, but two small birds were found, also lizards, mice, and a tiny cottontail rabbit. The small amount of vegetable matter consumed by the roadrunners appeared to consist of sour berries.

It must be admitted, however, that a few roadrunners do at times destroy a few young quail. Yet there is no evidence to support the common belief that roadrunners in general are persistent and customary predators on young quail; and in all the evidence both oral and written I have examined I have not found one single authentic instance of a roadrunner's having destroyed quail eggs. It may be that occasionally a roadrunner does eat quail eggs. But there are numerous instances of the destruction of mice, large wood rats, and various kinds of snakes by the bird—and snakes and rats are undoubtedly much more destructive of quail eggs and young quail than the roadrunners are themselves.

An old-time Mexican ranchero whom I met at Parral, in the state of Chihuahua, told me that country people in that region sometimes catch the paisano young, tame it, and utilize it to catch mice and rats.

Nature balances itself far better than man can ever balance it. The most roadrunners I have ever seen are in that part of Texas where the blue, or scaled, quail are admittedly more plentiful than anywhere else in the United States. I refer to the brush country of Southwest Texas centering around the counties of Duval, McMullen, La Salle, and Webb. By riding a day in some of the big pastures of this region in late summer of seasonable years a man might count a thousand blue quail, many bob whites, and easily a hundred paisanos. In the sand hills north and east of these counties, still in the brush country, bob whites used to abound by the thousands— are yet plentiful on some protected land—along with many, many paisanos.

You will not find the most colts and the most panthers in the same pasture, or the most lions and the most lambs. You will not find the most shotgun hunters and the most quail in the same pasture.

And what if the paisano is now and then directly responsible for one less quail to shoot at? He is a poor sportsman whose only interest in wild life is something to kill. How much more interesting and delightful is a country where a variety of wild life abounds! If it were necessary to choose between ten quail and no paisanos, or nine quail and one paisano, not many people who have any response towards nature or capacity for being delighted by the countryside would hesitate to choose the latter. The value of the roadrunner to the farmer as an insect destroyer need not be dwelt upon.

A few years ago a rancher named John Henderson who was trying to raise young turkeys on Honey Creek in Kerr County, Texas, began missing several from his bunch. Taking his shotgun, he one day followed a flock to the creek. He

151

saw a huge bullfrog leap out of the water, snap a little turkey up, and dive back into the water. He waited, and before long the bullfrog reappeared. He shot him, dissected him, and found the freshly swallowed turkey inside the frog. One swallow does not make a summer. Bullfrogs in general cannot be considered as destroyers of young turkeys. There are many individual variations among roadrunners just as there are among horses, men, and other kinds of animals.

Once while watching at a dirt tank on a ranch in Webb County, I saw a paisano that came up to drink peck at a frog, which escaped. A Mexican told me that the day preceding he had seen a paisano catch a small frog, beat it to death on the ground, and swallow it. Yet paisanos are characteristic of a country generally devoid of frogs, and certainly they are not generally frog-catchers. At a well not ten miles away from the one just mentioned, I saw half a dozen paisanos running around and around on the rim of a circular water trough, trying to reach down for a drink. The water was too low. Out in the middle of the trough, which was about eight feet in diameter, floated a good-sized board attached to the valve-float; this board was half covered with frogs. Not a paisano had sense enough to jump to the board and drink from it, and no paisano had the least intention of catching a frog.

I placed a dead mesquite limb in the trough so that one end of it went down into the water while the other rested on the rim. Not one had sense enough to walk down the limb to water. Two or three paisanos were at the same time running around on the tin roof of the cistern that fed the trough, trying to get at water. The saying in Southwest Texas, "as crazy as a paisano," seemed here well founded, although in some ways the bird certainly is not "crazy." Paisanos cannot swim at all and they frequently drown in cement troughs and cisterns.

I estimated there were probably a hundred paisanos within a radius of half a mile of the cement trough. On August 9 I discovered near it a nest up about ten feet in a mesquite tree. On my horse I could watch the old bird feeding her young. There were three nestlings, two about ready to leave, and a third less mature. The parent bird fed them exactly in rotation, exclusively on grasshoppers, as long as I watched, which was about an hour, the provider at the end of that time disappearing. She—or he—needed a rest. A youngster would open its mouth wide; the old one would poke grasshopper-laden bill down the orifice and hold it there until the morsel was swallowed. Then she would vol-plane down to the ground and scoot up into another mesquite or fly directly from the nest into another tree. The ground about was entirely shadowed by mesquites. She was catching most of her grasshoppers in the mesquites among the leaves. From a point of vantage she would cock her head this way and that until she located an insect, fly softly to a spot near it, and thence make a swift dart. Usually she caught, but sometimes the grasshopper escaped. From her position up in a tree she could see grasshoppers flying and lighting. If she located one lighting on the ground, the way she volplaned and nabbed it was a pretty sight. She never missed a grass-hopper on the ground as she sometimes missed one among the leaves.

Within a few rods of this paisano nest I saw five or six dove nests on which the doves were peacefully brooding, and I saw a little mocking-bird just out of its nest. The doves and mocking-birds did not seem to regard the paisanos as enemies. I saw a paisano make a pass at a rusty lizard, on a tree trunk, and miss it; the paisano seemed to expect this.

I have seen dozens of green lizards in the bills of paisanos but never a rusty lizard. There is a very tall tale about a roadrunner in California that kept a hill full of lizards growing tails for him to eat. This paisano discovered that a lizard would, unlike Little Bo Peep's sheep, leave its tail behind it if the tail was snapped up, and would then grow a new tail just as good to swallow as the original.

An astounding revelation of the voracity of the bird is given by G. M. Sutton in an account of two pet roadrunners, "Titania and Oberon," in his book *Birds in the Wilderness.* He tells how they manage to swallow horned frogs. The paisano digests rapidly. He will begin swallowing a snake inches long and after he has got a certain portion of it down must wait for the digestive juices to act before he can swallow further. Thus he may have to go about for hours with a part of the snake dangling out of his mouth before he can get it all down. He is truly, to use the phrase out of an old folk rhyme, a "greedy gut."

When Doctor H. A. Pilsbury of Philadelphia came to Texas and Mexico a few years ago hunting snails, I told him he should throw in with the paisanos. He didn't understand what I meant. I explained how in Southwest Texas—and probably elsewhere—the paisano picks up a snail, breaks the shell on a rock, and then eats the meat; how he will bring snail after snail to the rock he has selected as a meat-block, or table, to break it, passing scores of other rocks on his way; how sometimes at one of these rocks, or maybe a hard bit of bare ground, more than a cupful of broken snail shells may be picked up. Doctor Pilsbury replied that, so far as he knew, there was but one other bird in the world that eats snails in this way. That is an English thrush, and the places where the thrushes collect the snails are called "thrush altars." Should the paisano have an altar, a chuck wagon, or a *mesa?*

Eggs and Habits

The average clutch of eggs seems to be from four to six, but two or three often compose the number, and there are records of up to twelve. As soon as the first egg is laid, incubation begins, and the succeeding eggs are laid irregularly. In consequence, the birds hatch off over such a long period of time that the first fledgling will sometimes be ready to leave the nest before the last egg is pipped. After the second or third bird is hatched, the adults—for the cock is said to do a share in setting—spend little daylight time on the nest, the body heat of the young sufficing to keep the eggs warm. According to Mrs. Bruce Reid, the male bird takes care of the first young ones to come off the nest, while the female feeds the last nestlings. Mrs. Reid had a pet male three years old that adopted and took charge of feeding two baby-roadrunners she brought home; he favored in many ways the female of this pair of young ones.

The nest is loosely built in an old log fence, in a Spanish dagger, up in a mesquite, within a clump of brush, etc. Owing to the long neck and longer tail of the bird, one sitting on a nest appears to be cramped, but perhaps isn't.

Little seems to be known about the mating maneuvers of the paisano. Do they pair for life? My brother, Elrich Dobie, who ranches in Webb and LaSalle counties, told me that twice he had seen a male paisano mount a female, and in each instance with a worm in his mouth that he reached around and gave to the female. There are more variations in the calls made by the bird than many people realize, and during mating season the calls are rich.

While not to be classed as migratory, roadrunners do, I believe, shift their grounds to an extent in the winter. In August of 1936 I counted between 75 and 100 in a day on the old Buckley ranch near Cotulla, Texas. I could not be sure of the count, for some of the birds were certainly met twice. The next December on a deer hunt on the same ranch I saw only one bird during the day. Mexicans said the paisanos were down in the thickest thickets, but I was not convinced. A man who has a stock-farm out a short distance from San Marcos says that a particular roadrunner stayed on his place, often appearing about the barn and corrals, for several years. It would disappear during the winter and reappear with early spring.

Paisanos are found far from water and in waterless deserts. Some observers have thought water not essential to them. This may well be in places where they have adapted themselves to desert conditions, especially since they eat animal food containing a high per cent of fluid. In Sonora there are deer that almost never drink water, although the same deer in other parts of the world drink more or less regularly. Where water is available, however, roadrunners are thirsty drinkers in the hot summer. In Southwest Texas they are exceedingly methodical and regular in coming to water. One time while I was watching a gasoline engine pumping water for cattle during the dog days of August, a period when the wind habitually fails to blow enough to turn windmills, I noticed how a particular paisano came every day about a quarter of twelve o'clock to drink. He was as regular as the sun.

The bird has a great deal of curiosity and is easily domesticated if taken young. One will hop into the open door of a house and stand there a long time, looking this way and that. Perhaps he has an idea that some shade-loving creature suited to his diet is in the house. He will come up to a camp to investigate in the same way. I never tire of watching one of these birds dart down a trail or road, suddenly throw on the brakes by hoisting his tail, stand for a minute dead still except for panting and cocking his head to one

156

side and then to the other, and then suddenly streak out again. The way he raises and lowers the plumage on his lustrous-feathered head while he goes *crut, crut, crut* with his vocal organs is an endless fascination. He must surely be the most comical bird of America. He will go through more antics and cut up more didos in an hour than a parrot can be taught in a lifetime.

How the idea that he cannot fly at all got started, I cannot imagine. Down a hill or a mountain he can volplane for long distances. Frequently one will fly up into a tree to get a wide view. Of course, however, he is essentially a ground bird. His speed, like nearly everything else connected with him, has been greatly exaggerated. Any good horse can outrun one on a considerable stretch. Walter Fry of the Sequoia National Park, California, is quoted as saying that a roadrunner he was chasing in an automobile attained the speed of 26 miles an hour. Bailey's *Birds of New Mexico* gives his top speed, tested by automobile, as fifteen miles an hour. Running down a path ahead of a buggy or a horseman, the roadrunner often seems to enjoy the exercise as much as a pup enjoys chasing a chicken or a calf. While speeding, he stretches out almost flat. Sometimes he falls in behind a traveler and follows down a trail. He enjoys a dust bath. He can stand terrific heat, but on hot days he likes to pause in the shade, even though it be nothing but the shadow of a three-inch mesquite fence post.

Killers of Rattlesnakes

That paisanos, singly and in pairs, kill rattlesnakes is a fact established beyond all doubt, although folk-lore amassed around the subject has made ornithologists slow to admit the fact. One vice of erudition is that it tends to patronize popular knowledge, great-natured men of science like Audubon and W. H. Hudson being exceptions to the general tendency.

157

In the fall of 1928 near Robstown, Texas, some dogs over-took a roadrunner unable to get out of the way because of a rattlesnake in its mouth. They killed the bird before men could stop them. After a photograph was taken of the dead bird with the snake dangling out of its bill, the snake was extracted and measured. It was eighteen inches long and had four or five rattles.

For many years I have hoped to come upon a paisano-rattlesnake combat — just as I have hoped to come upon two buck deer with antlers locked in mortal combat. The witness-ing of either phenomenon depends so much upon chance that only a few individuals among many who spend their lives out of doors happen upon the scene at the right time. I have questioned scores of *hombres del campo* — men of range and countryside — about paisano-rattlesnake fights, and I have the testimony of several whose word cannot be doubted.

In October, 1932, Bob Dowe, of Eagle Pass, a strong-bodied and strong-minded man who had had a great deal of experience on ranches on both sides of the Rio Grande, told me that he once saw a paisano kill a rattlesnake about three and a half feet long. The fight was in a cow pen. The bird in its maneuvers raised a great amount of dust. With wings extended and dragging in the dust, it would run at the snake, aiming at its head. The snake struck blindly, several times hitting the paisano's wings, without effect, of course. Finally the bird pecked a hole in the snake's head and punctured the brain. It ate the brain but nothing else. The shrike, or butcher bird, is said to thus eat only the brains of small birds it kills, which may sometimes be seen hanging intact on thorns or the barbs of barbed wire fences — a manner of wasteful selection employed also by plainsmen who shot down giant buffaloes merely for the tongues and by those ancient gour-mands who banqueted on nightingale tongues.

I have heard of the paisano's killing little chickens and

158

eating only the brain. I do not know this to be a fact, however. I know that on the ranch of my boyhood and youth in Live Oak County we had many chickens and many paisanos, which often came among the chickens, big and little; the chickens never seemed to pay the paisanos any more attention than they paid the blackbirds, doves and quail. Between the pens at the stables and the branding pens was about a hundred yards of old log fence that had been built as part of a little horse pasture before the advent of barbed wire. In this old fence there were paisano nests every year. Snakes — particularly chicken snakes, but also sometimes coachwhips and bull snakes—ate eggs and little chickens; coyotes were a constant menace; but we never thought of the paisanos as being destructive to the chickens. The snake's most vulnerable part, his head, reminds me of a saying made by Victoriano Huerta while he was president of the southern republic: *"Mexico es come un serpiente; toda la vida es en la cabeza."* (Mexico is like a serpent; all the life is in its head — the capital city.)

And this brings me to Don Alberto Guajardo, of Piedras Negras, one of the best nature observers I have ever met. "I have never seen a paisano kill a rattlesnake," he said, in February, 1935, "but not long ago a boy on my ranch told me he had seen this thing so often reported by others. I asked him many questions to trap him in falsehood. In the end I was convinced that he was telling the truth. The boy said he first heard the paisano and then, looking about, saw the combat very near. With outstretched wings the paisano was making passes at the snake, evidently with intention of infuriating him. After many violent lunges, the snake subsided. Then with a swift leap the bird lit on the neck of the snake, seeming to hold it in his claws, while he pecked at the head two or three times. The writhing body of the snake made the bird leap away. A drop of blood showed on the head of the snake,

159

and now it tried to hide its head under its body. Again the paisano attacked. This time he killed the snake. He ate only the brains."

Mrs. Bruce Reid, of Port Arthur, who has raised several roadrunners as well as many other birds and who has supplied much information to the Biological Survey, tells of having witnessed two paisano-rattlesnake combats. In each instance, the snake's head was bruised and bloody. One rattler, about three feet long, sought refuge in some cactus, but the paisano, as hot after it as a hound after a wildcat, got to it. In its writhings, the rattler brushed an irregular line of dead cactus leaves about its body — a circumstance that might account for the tradition of a cactus corral.

Sometimes the paisano is described as giving a "war dance" about the rattler to confuse and infuriate him. Wild turkeys are said to make attacks, occasionally, on rattlesnakes in much the same manner.

In the spring of 1932 Ellen Schulz Quillin, botanist, something of a naturalist, and director of the excellent Witte Museum in San Antonio, was quoted in an article appearing in the San Antonio *Express* as saying that while the paisano is an avid destroyer of field pests, there was little foundation for the belief that it kills rattlesnakes. Within a few days she received a letter from Alfred Toepperwein, rancher of Bulverde, Bexar County. Toepperwein wrote that he had shot many of the birds while riding in his pasture but that a single experience had put a stop to all shooting. His letter as quoted in the *Express* of March 17, 1932, reads:

"One day I saw one of the birds, feathers turned forward like an angry deer turns its hair, jumping up and down, back and forth. I paid no attention, but pulled my .45 and fired, missing the bird barely by an inch. The bird, not a bit frightened, kept its feathers up and kept jumping towards the same place. Then the rattlesnake story I had heard several times came to my memory. I went to the place and found a rattle-snake almost dead. I have killed no more chaparral birds since then."

I might adduce further evidence, considered by me un-impeachable, from Nat Gunter, rancher at Balmorhea, Texas; John Wildenthal, deputy sheriff at Cotulla, Texas, and other men, but I will conclude the testimony by a quotation from *Time* magazine, March 7, 1938, which reproduced also a pic-ture, not fabricated, showing a roadrunner about to leap at a rattler, more than twice as long as the bird, with head and forepart raised to strike. "Last week," the article runs, "a full-length documentary film on Mexican animals, produced by Brothers Stacy and Horace Woodard, made the road-runner-rattlesnake story a little less tall but no less telling. *The Adventures of Chico* shows ten-year-old Goatherd Chico taking his siesta, guarded by his roadrunner pet. A rattle-snake approaches. Without hesitation the bird attacks, head feathers fanned and wings tensely spread. Like a matador, it lures the snake into striking, easily swings out of reach. Like a matador, it waits and feints till the enemy tires, then kills with swift skill."

The filmers of this scene spent a year in Mexico taking animal pictures. The relation of the boy Chico to the bird may easily have been arranged, but the fight between snake and bird admits of no faking. The story of how a sleeping shepherd awakes to find a rattlesnake threatening him and is saved by the timely intervention of the snake's inveterate enemy is common. Jack H. Lee in his book of verse, *West of Powder River* (New York, 1933), has a ballad relating the incident.

An old Mexican in northern Coahuila told me that one time he found four paisano eggs in a nest and put them under a hen and hatched them out. They grew up to be pets around his lone *jacal* (cabin) out in the chaparral. One time after

161

dinner, he said, he went to take a siesta under a runty mesquite tree not far from the *jacal*. He was sleeping soundly when the noise made by the paisanos awoke him. Impatiently, he gave them a scare; then he discovered that they had three medium-sized rattlesnakes cornered. He was convinced that the birds had saved his life. He did not explain why there were not four rattlesnakes instead of just three.

Leaving man out of the picture entirely, the truth is being proven, and there is no reason why ornithologists should henceforth use the words "seems," "perhaps," or "it is generally said" in modifying remarks about lethal combats between paisanos and rattlesnakes.

II. Folklore

The Corral of Thorns

If I were writing an article strictly scientific, I should at this point drop the rattlesnake; but any animal is interesting to man not only for the facts about him but for what human beings associated with the animal have taken to be the facts. "No man," Mary Austin says, "has ever really entered into the heart of any country until he has adopted or made up myths about its familiar objects." Hardly any established fact about the paisano is as familiar to the public as some form of the story about the bird's corralling a rattlesnake with cactus joints and then either killing it or making it kill itself. The bird is certainly more interesting for this commonly believed and more commonly told story. It has appeared various times in print, nowhere so divertingly told as by The Old Cattleman in Alfred Henry Lewis's *Wolfville*, which account I borrowed for *On the Open Range*. Other forms of the story appear in other books for children: to cite two recent ones, *Indians of the Pueblos*, by Therese O. Deming, and *Thinking,*

Speaking and Writing (Book Two), by Jameson, Clark and Veit.

Nor am I prepared to deny that paisanos ever corral rattle-snakes. Perhaps they could. The act would be no more of a strain on nature than the building of a web by a spider to entrap a fly. It is claimed that snakes hear through the ground and that a sleeping rattlesnake could not be corralled without his becoming aroused. I do not know. The roadrunner runs lightly. But I make no argument, no denial. The stories are interesting. They are part of the history of the most interest-ing bird of the Southwest. Some of the narratives are very circumstantial — as all good narratives must be.

In May, 1933, I was introduced to E. V. Anaya, a practicer in international law of Mexico City. He was reared on a hacienda in Sonora, where he was associated with Opata Indians. He is as swart as a desert Indian himself and as decisive as Mussolini. The Indians and Mexicans of Sonora call the paisano *churella,* he said.

"Have you ever seen one kill a rattlesnake?" he asked. "No? Well, I have — once."

"I was out gathering pitayas," he went on. The pitaya, or pitalla, is a cactus fruit. "It was in the month of May — the month of pitayas. I was just a boy, about 1908. I was with an Opata Indian.

"Just as we got to the top of a mesa, the Indian very cau-tiously beckoned me to come nearer. Then when I was close to him, he whispered, 'See the churella.'

" 'Churella,' I replied. 'What of it?' The bird is so common in that country that little attention is usually paid to it.

" 'This one is killing a rattlesnake,' the Indian spoke softly. 'Let us watch.'

"We crept up silently, until we were within twelve or fifteen yards of the churella. A rattlesnake lay coiled on the ground, out in a little open space, apparently asleep. The churella had already gathered a great many joints of the cholla cactus and had outlined a corral around the snake. The corral was maybe three feet in diameter.

"The churella was working swiftly. Cholla was growing all around us and the joints were lying everywhere on the ground. The bird would carry a joint in its long beak without getting pricked. He built the little corral up, laying one joint on top of another, until it was maybe four inches high. Then he dropped a joint right on top of the sleeping snake. The snake moved, and when he did, the spines found the openings under his scales. The snake became frantic and went to slashing against the corral. That made it more frantic. Then the churella attacked it on the head and had little trouble in killing it. The spines made it practically defenseless."

If a roadrunner were going to use any kind of cactus to corral or torment a rattlesnake with, cholla joints would surely be best suited to the purpose. Each joint is so spined that if one single thorn takes hold of an object and the object moves the least bit, another and then several other thorns will dig in. Instead of throwing off the cholla joint, movement causes the one thorn in the flesh to act as a lever for giving more thorns entrance. In the bad cholla country of Sonora I have ridden a native horse, wary of the thorns, that, nevertheless, caught several in his pastern. Then the only thing to do was to dismount, get a stick, and with it jerk the cholla joint directly out. I have seen a cave in that same country with enough cholla joints heaped in it to fill a freight car. They had been placed there by rats. The Papago Indians used to dispose of their dead by laying the body on open ground and then heaping cholla over it — a thorough protection against all beasts of prey.

Snakes, rattlesnakes included, eat rats. All kinds of rats in all parts of the Southwest build about their nests a defense of thorns against snakes and other enemies. The rattlesnake

164

may not, as folk theory once held, be sensitive to the tickling of a hair rope; but he can't go like a shadow through an armor of thorns.

Not long after Lawyer Anaya of Mexico City told me his story of the churella, the cholla, and the rattlesnake, I went to see General Roberto Morelos Zaragoza in the city of San Luís Potosí. An ardent hunter and outdoors man, he was issuing monthly a small magazine called *Aire Libre* (Open Air), made up of hunting and fishing chronicles. The general's primary interest in wild life was that of a killer, but he was naturally alert, and had made many observations on the habits of animals.

He called the paisano a *faisán* (pheasant) — the name the bird goes by around San Luís Potosí. "Yes," he said, "with my own eyes I have seen a *faisán* kill a very large rattlesnake. The *faisán* took a tuna (the Indian fig, or apple) from a *cardón* cactus, dropped it on the neck of the snake, and while the snake was maddened by the thorns pecked it to death on top of the head."

An old German mining engineer named Engelbert Brokhurst, widely traveled, learned, observant, and cranky, whom I met in Mazatlan, told me that Indians of the West Coast of Mexico regard the paisano as a sacred bird and will not kill it. They all say that the bird corrals sleeping rattlesnakes and then torments them to death with thorns.

The evidence, however, is by no means all from Indians and Mexicans. *Black Range Tales* (New York, 1936) is a book of reminiscences by an old-time prospector and miner named James A. McKenna, of New Mexico. "One spring in Lake Valley," he relates, "my partner and I watched a pair of roadrunners. Morning after morning we met them outside the tunnel where we worked. Not far from the mouth of the tunnel a rattlesnake used to climb on a rock to take a sleep in the early morning sun. [They were out-of-the-ordinary out-

165

doors men not to kill it.] It soon became plain to us that the roadrunners had spotted the rattlesnake. One morning we saw them making a corral of cholla joints and thorns around the snake. How quietly they worked until the crude circle was nearly three inches high! Then both birds ran with a strange cry towards the cholla corral, waking up the rattlesnake, which struck instantly. Hundreds of fine sharp thorns were buried in the tender underside of the snake's throat. The more he twisted and turned, the deeper the spines of the cholla worked into his neck. After a half-hour of writhing, he lay still. The roadrunners hung around long enough to make sure he was dead; then they hacked him to pieces, which they carried off to feed their young. Prospectors always keep on the lookout for rattlesnakes if they take note of a pair of roadrunners in the vicinity of the camp."

Yet some critic has spoiled this story by claiming that a paisano does not have enough force in his beak to tear the flesh from a rattlesnake carcass.

Something of a variation in the use of cactus comes in an account written by Hampton McNeill of the Texas Panhandle. Hunting quail one day, McNeill heard "some kind of unfamiliar chuckling" going on just over a small mound. He stepped up on top of the mound, and there a "chaparral and a rattlesnake were fighting for life and death. The snake was completely encircled by cactus leaves. Its head had been pierced so many times by the cactus thorns that a match-head could hardly have been placed anywhere on it without covering a thorn hole." The narrator probably had no magnifying glass to look at the holes. Remember, however, that the prickly pear in the Panhandle grows low and scrawny; the leaves (known to botany as pads) are not strongly jointed.

"The chaparral would run up to a cactus bush, take a good hold on a leaf with its bill, shake the leaf loose, and then return to the scene of battle. Using this thorny leaf as a shield, the chaparral would rile the rattler into striking at him. After the snake had struck several times, the bird would lay the leaf down near the snake.

"The chaparral repeated this action several times. In the course of time, the rattler seemed to become completely exhausted, for he would no longer offer resistance when the chaparral returned with more cactus leaves. Having brought up two or three leaves without arousing the snake to action, he then disappeared in the sage brush. The snake was not dead, but I put him out of his misery."

Philip Ashton Rollins, in his generally excellent treatise, *The Cowboy*, describes still another mode of attack whereby the bird uses thorns but does not bother with a pen. "The chaparral-cock," he says, "might stop its hunt for bugs, seize in its bill a group of cactus thorns, spread its wings wide and low, and, running more speedily than could any race horse, dodging as elusively as does heat-lightning, drive those thorns squarely into the snake's open mouth, peck out both the beady eyes, and then resume the hunt for bugs." According to the *gente*, a paisano upon finding a rattlesnake charming a rabbit, slips up and jabs a cactus joint into the waiting jaws of the would-be killer.

The more usual end, perhaps, of the story of the rattler corralled by cactus spines is that narrated by The Old Cattleman in Alfred Henry Lewis' *Wolfville*. "At last comes the finish, and matters get dealt down to the turn. The rattlesnake suddenly crooks his neck, he's so plumb locoed with rage an' fear, an' socks his fangs into himself. That's the fact; bites himse'f, an' never lets up till he's dead."

I am not sure of final findings but I have been informed by scientific men that rattlesnake venom injected into the blood system of the very creature carrying the venom will be as deadly as in the blood system of any other animal. Such an end is not impossible. According to the tales, then, there

167

are three possible ways for the rattler to die after paisanos have corralled him. (1) He may bite himself to death; (2) he may have his brain punctured by the bird's beak just as it is sometimes punctured without benefit of the corral; (3) he may be brained by thorns themselves.

What would happen if a rattlesnake bit the paisano in a vital spot may be deduced from an account in a book first published in Cincinnati in 1847, by C. Donavan, *Adventures in Mexico*. During his captivity in the Mexican War, Donavan visited an extensive botanical garden near San Luís Potosí, and there became acquainted with *huaco* — the most celebrated herbal cure for snakebite in Mexico and the southern tip of Texas. The discovery of the medicinal qualities of *huaco*, Donavan learned from the natives, was attributed to a bird that "feeds upon snakes and reptiles." Indians in the far past noticed that after a combat with a snake the bird would "search for the herb and eat it." Thus they learned from the bird, which Donavan calls the guayaquil but which is patently the paisano, the "sure remedy" for snakebite.

From the paisano, too — perhaps — certain Indians of the Southwest took the idea of putting long fringes on their moccasins and leggins as a protection against snakebite, the fringes suggesting feathers to the snake. Indeed, the wands used to calm rattlesnakes in the Hopi snake dance are of feathers, though they are of the eagle, which preys on snakes.

Other Lore

The very track of the roadrunner has among some of the Pueblo Indians of New Mexico given the bird significance and protection. This track shows two toes pointed forward and two backward, and Indians duplicate it on the ground all about the tent of one of their dead so as to mislead evil spirits seeking the course taken by the departed soul. Again, an Indian mother will tie the bright feathers of a roadrunner on the cradle-board so as to confuse evil spirits that would trouble her child's mind. Here the feathers signify the track, which not only points two ways but is four-directioned like the Cross.

In his "Report" on New Mexico, printed by the United States Government in 1848 and containing much on the fauna and flora of the region, Lieutenant J. W. Albert inserts a curious note concerning the bird's toes. Although they are, he quotes an informer as saying, "disposed in opposite pairs, as in other species of the cuckoo family, yet the outer hind toe, being reversible and of great flexibility, is in either position (whether pointed forward or backward) aptly applied in climbing or perching as well as on the ground. Thus he at times pitches along the ground in irregular hops; again, when the outer hind toe is thrown forward, he runs smoothly and with such rapidity as always to be able to elude a dog in the chaparral without taking wings." Did anybody ever see paisano tracks with three toes pointing forward?

Certain of the Plains Indians hung the whole skin of the roadrunner — to them the medicine bird — over a lodge door to keep out henchmen of the Bad God. Before setting out on an expedition, a warrior would attach one or more paisano feathers to his person. At least one tribe of California Indians used the feathers for adorning their head-dress — probably with symbolic intent also.

An Austrian mining engineer I met in Mexico City told me that during many years of mule-back travel through mountains all over Mexico he had heard *mozos* — those indispensable muleteer guides and servants — in different parts of the country say that the *corre camino* is a guide for mankind, that if a lost man will find one of the birds and follow it, it will lead him to a trail. The *corre camino* not only fancies trails but follows them for the tumble-bugs (beetles)

169

and other insects that come to feed on the droppings of pack animals passing over the trail.

One time while I was crossing the Sierra Madre from the Pacific Ocean to the city of Oaxaca, I saw three Indian men at a stream. Their shirtless torsos revealed them as fine physical specimens, and after I had, with permission, taken a picture of them, I asked which of the three was the *jefe* (chief). The two end men pointed to the center man. I gave him a package of cigarettes and rode on, trotting to catch up with my companions and the pack mules. The *jefe* kept at my heels. He had held this position for perhaps half an hour when I noticed a roadrunner just ahead of me about to cross the trail from right to left. The Indian picked up two or three rocks and chunked at the bird with intense earnestness, missing him, however.

I was surprised, and asked the Indian why he wanted to kill a bird that brought good luck. He said something in reply that I could not understand. He could speak only a few incoherent Spanish words and talked in his own dialect. Arriving in Oaxaca, I had considerable conversation with a savant named Paul Van de Velde. He told me that the Indians of that region claimed the bird brought good luck if it crossed the road from left to right but bad luck if from right to left. I remembered then that the bird my Indian escort tried so earnestly to kill was crossing from right to left. He was trying to prevent bad luck from coming to me.

Yet in many places in Mexico the bird is regarded as benevolent without respect to the direction in which it may be traveling. "Look, *patrón*," I have had a *mozo* say to me in the morning, "look at that paisano over there. We'll have good traveling today." A paisano that stays about the house is often cherished by Mexicans as much as the swallow building its nest under the shed roof — the swallow that always betokens good fortune. Among Mexicans on the Texas border

170

the paisano takes the place of the stork in bringing babies into the world.

The bird is a true *cristiano*. One time Mr. Boyles of the Witte Museum in San Antonio, while out hunting specimens, stopped at a shack occupied by some poor white people. The woman here told him that nearly every day they saw one or more paisanos stop at noon and bow their heads to pray. "Is that what the paisanos are doing when they make bows?" Mr. Boyles asked. "Yes," the woman replied, "the Mexicans all believe the paisano stops at noon to pray, no matter where he is." The American woman's expression as she gave this information showed she wanted mighty bad to believe the Mexicans.

As has already been said, the very virtues of the bird may at times prove his death. The Tarahumare Indians of the Sierra Madre, perhaps the most remarkable runners in the world, regard the flesh of the paisano as not only wholesome but conducive to speed and endurance.

The eating of a paisano roasted over the coals is supposed by some Mexicans to cure the itch. This is a local cure based on a legend that centuries and centuries ago a tramp came to an Indian village, the inhabitants of which welcomed and fed him. Before long an epidemic of severe itch broke out among them. The medicine men finally examined the body of the tramp and found it covered with itch. He had brought the curse. They turned him into a paisano, killed, roasted and ate him — and were all cured.

The paisano cure for boils is known all over the Southwest and Mexico. The fifteen-year-old son of the owner of a big ranch in West Texas had been with the cow outfit for two months. Then he became so plagued with Job's worst affliction that he had to be carried to the ranch in a car. One of the *gente* went out and shot two paisanos. The boy ate them fried and got well of the boils almost at once. Boiling, though, is

171

usually better than frying; but any way taken, paisano meat beats sarsaparilla all hollow as a blood purifier.

Mexican women grow flowers no matter if their home is only a box car housing a railroad construction crew; perhaps it is fortunate for the paisano that these cherishers of flowers do not set out many shrubs and trees. If you want such to grow, "kill a paisano, cut out the entrails, and put them at the bottom of the hole, just under the roots."

In northern Mexico I have several times heard of the wonderful fighting cock, high jumping and lightning-quick with his spurs, produced by crossing a paisano with a game chicken. But I have never been able to come upon this bird—just as I have never been able to come upon the marvelous hybrid resulting from a cross between a ram and a sow. A young man named Ramón who traveled with me into the desert of the Bolsón de Mapimí claimed to have once owned a very, very superior fighting cock out of an egg laid by a game hen fertilized by a pet paisano. He kept the origin of this extraordinary *gallo* a secret, he said, and won many bets off him. I might have been more inclined to credit Ramón's account had he not asserted that a paisano when run down will turn over on its back, hiding its head in grass, and stick up its rusty legs so that they appear to be dry weed-stalks or twigs. Yet, after all, why shouldn't a paisano use its legs as camouflage? One scared off a nest has been known to try to toll the intruder away by simulating a broken leg, as some flying birds simulate broken wings.

An even more wonderful bird than the paisano game cock is the *pájaro cu.*[1] Nobody claims to have ever seen the *pájaro cu.* In the beginning of things he was naked, and all the birds held a kind of convention at which the owl proposed that

---

[1]Riley Aiken tells the story of "El Pájaro Cú" in *Puro Mexicano* (Publication of the Texas Folk-Lore Society, 1935), pp. 19-20; I tell it in my book, *Tongues of the Monte*, pp. 100-103.

each bird chip in a feather or two and thus make up a decent covering for the poor naked one. The peafowl objected to the proposal, arguing that a suit of so many colors would make the bird impossibly vain. But King Eagle, overruling the objection, ordered the feathers donated, provided two birds would stand as sponsors for the *pájaro cu* and guarantee his decent conduct. The paisano and the owl volunteered as sponsors. The new plumage was brighter and more varied in colors than a double rainbow. It went to the *pájaro cu's* head, and he offended many birds, especially the peafowl, by his vanity. King Eagle called another convention of the birds to consider the case, but the *pájaro cu* was not present.

Then the sponsors, the paisano and the owl, were ordered to produce him. They could not find him. They have been looking for him ever since. The owl at night calls *whu, whu, whu,* the closest he can get to *cu, cu, cu,* and the paisano runs up and down the roads by day, looking this way and that way, and shooting out like the sounds of a *matraca,* his *cru, cru, cru,* the nearest he can get to *cu, cu, cu.* A good deal of the time, though, he seems to say *crut, crut, crut,* rolling and trilling and twirling the *r* sound with such mastery that you know Spanish is his native tongue.

Although not at all a pheasant, early Spaniards are said on good authority to have called the paisano *faisán réal.* And a "royal pheasant" indeed this bird that now runs the roads once considered himself, as Jovita González[2] heard the story among the border people. He had proud ways, as he still has at times, walking in the evening time with crest erected, long tail switching from side to side, lifting one foot deliberately before the other, and often raising himself to a stately height. He would not speak to such humble birds as the sparrows. The dove was too modest for him to notice,

---

[2]"Tales and Songs of the Texas-Mexicans." by Jovita González, in *Man, Bird and Beast,* Pub. No. VIII of the Texas Folk-Lore Society. Austin, 1930, pp. 92-93.

and the wren too pert. But all the bright, lofty and noble birds he addressed with cousinly familiarity. It was "Good morning, Paisano Zenzontle, and how is your Lordship," as he noticed a mockingbird singing on a high twig, or "How are you, Paisano?" ruffling his throat feathers to vie with the colors of the cardinal he thus addressed. Even the eagle was *paisano* to him.

One day while this king of the bird world had his lords and nobles together discussing grave matters of state, the vain fellow who considered himself a "royal pheasant" stalked into their presence without announcement, cocked his head over with the same ceremony he would use in looking at an earthworm crawl out of moist ground, and said, "How fares my countryman? And, my *paisanos* all, how are you?"

The eagle was simply furious at such familiarity. He screamed, "Out of my presence, you low-born thing of the ground. Never again presume to be a *faisán*. Henceforth stay on the ground where you belong. Forget to try to fly. Feed on tarantulas, scorpions, and beetles. Go."

The poor bird tried to fly from the courtroom, but could not. His wings had lost their strength. He had to run out of the room like a chicken. He has belonged to the ground ever since. And the name *paisano* that both people and birds call him by now is a mockery of the presumption he so long ago paid for.

Yet people like the paisano. When one man in this bird's wide range meets another that he feels warm sympathy for, he may say, "We speak the same language." But, if there is great gusto in the correspondence of spirits, he will say, "*Nosotros somos paisanos*—we are fellow countrymen—we belong to the same soil." And we true paisanos of mankind include in our kinship the paisanos of birdkind.

This essay on the roadrunner appeared, somewhat abbreviated, in the *Natural History Magazine*, New York, September, 1939.

CONTRIBUTORS

Charles Flinn Arrowood, Professor of History and Philosophy of Education in the University of Texas and author of several books in his field, confesses to the hobby of gathering and telling anecdotes illustrative of American social history.

Merrill Bishop, author of *Chromotrophes* and other verse, is Assistant Director of Education in the San Antonio Public Schools.

R. B. Blake, of Nacogdoches, has never, so far as the public knows, written a detective novel. Perhaps he is too guileless for that. No G man or Scotland Yard sleuth, however, ever surpassed him as a detective in gathering stray evidence and putting it together to make out a case. He has long been interested in early Texas history and is one of the authorities in the Texas State Historical Association.

Ruth Dodson, of Mathis, Texas, is a Tejana and a Texian from who laid the chunk. She contributed "Folk-Curing Among the Mexicans" to Publications No. X *(Tone the Bell Easy)* of the Texas Folk-Lore Society—a kind of postscript to her unique booklet, *Don Pedro Jaramillo,* which, in addition to setting forth the life and ways of that famous *curandero* (medicine man), assembles a remarkable collection of remedies and miracles. It is written in Spanish.

Marcelle Lively Hamer, treasurer of the Texas Folk-Lore Society and Assistant in the Texas Collection of the Library of the University of Texas, wrote her Master's thesis on the subject of anecdotes.

Charlie Jeffries lives on a farm, which he works, near Winkler, Navarro County. He is an active member of the Texas State Historical Association; he has contributed to the *Southwest Review;* his article on "Early Texas Architecture" in *Bunker's Monthly,* June, 1928, is the best thing written on that subject. Years ago he took a trial vacation from farming to come to Austin and mix in the stir of culture. He founded a magazine called *The Aclavache,* issued one number, and retired. The soil of rusticity clings to him as to few other men who write about Texas.

Mrs. Winnifred Thalman Kupper, who teaches in the San Antonio schools, has written a book—not yet published—made up largely of the autobiography of one of the pioneer English sheepmen operating in Texas and to the west. This sheepman, Robert Maudslay, is her uncle. She belongs in the sheep tradition and is delightfully determined on seeing that sheep share some of the glamor heretofore monopolized by cows.

Edward G. Rohrbough came to Texas in 1937 from West Virginia to learn and write about Jim Bowie of Bowie knife fame. He wrote his Master's thesis in the University of Texas on Bowie and is now tutor of English in that institution.

Dan Storm, sometimes a resident of Austin, sometimes of New Mexico, and at other times a lore-gathering philosopher and listener sniffing the air in other parts of the Southwest, has come to be one of the most appreciated contributors to the books issued yearly by the Texas Folk-Lore Society. His tale of "The Wonderful Chirrionera" in *Puro Mexicano* (1935) and collection of tales about "The Little Animals of Mexico" in *Coyote Wisdom* (1938) are notable examples of folk-telling.

R. A. Tsanoff, who is Professor of Philosophy in the Rice Institute, of Houston, is one of the outstanding American philosophers and writers on philosophic subjects. His intense—he is an intense man—interest in fairy tales probably led to his election as president of the Texas Folk-Lore Society in 1938. That year his fine essay, "Philosophy in Folk-Lore," appeared in the volume, *Coyote Wisdom*, issued by the Society. "Folk-Lore and Tradition in a Growing Society" was delivered at the dedication of the San Jacinto Memorial Museum, April, 1939.

It has been a long time since 1925. In that year the Texas Folk-Lore Society issued Volume IV of its Publications. One contribution in it, "A Mexican Popular Ballad," by **W. A. Whatley,** remains outstanding not only for the ballad but for the setting provided by

176

the author. Mr. Whatley was reared on a big ranch in Mexico and talks Mexican like a native. He is now in the printing business in Austin.

Yanh-na-bah is registered in the University of Arizona under the name of **Elma Smith.** She prefers her Navajo name, however, which means "Becoming Victorious." Her attention was directed to the Texas Folk-Lore Society by Miss Frances Gillmor, author of the beautifully sincere and interesting book, *Traders to the Navajos.*

William Physick Zuber was born in Georgia in 1822 and eight years later accompanied his family to Texas, where, after several shiftings about, they settled near what is now Roan's Prairie, in Grimes County. In his sixteenth year William P. Zuber enlisted in the Texas Revolutionary Army. Considered too young to fight, and, moreover, having only a worthless gun to fight with, he was guarding the baggage while Houston's men won the battle of San Jacinto. Later he served in various Indian campaigns and, during the Civil War, was in the Texas Cavalry. In his later years, his memory always tenacious, he spent much time corresponding and writing. His manuscript, "Zuber's Eighty Years in Texas," about six hundred pages of legible script, is in the Archives of the State Library at Austin. Another long manuscript, largely of biographical sketches, is in the possession of Mr. Earl Van Dale, of Amarillo. He died in 1913.

TWENTY-FIFTH ANNUAL MEETING OF THE
TEXAS FOLK-LORE SOCIETY

For its twenty-fifth annual meeting the Texas Folk-Lore Society met in Houston, April 21 and 22, 1939. Its function the first day was to attend—in so far as members elected to do so—the elaborate exercises sponsored by the San Jacinto Museum of History Association in dedicating the San Jacinto Museum. On the morning of April 21, R. A. Tsanoff, President of the Society, delivered the principal address at the San Jacinto tower, his subject being "Folk-Lore and Tradition in a Growing Society." That beautiful and noble essay is printed in this volume. On the evening of April 21 members of the Society joined in the dinner sponsored by the San Jacinto Museum of History Association at the Rice Hotel, Doctor Edgar Odell Lovett, of the Rice Institute, presiding and Peter Molyneaux, editor of the *Texas Weekly,* piling up with his wonted facility mountains of statistics on the subject of "Texas, a Heritage and a Trust." Although he did not mean it that way, Don Pedro's prophecy that the country would lose in population if the policy of the New Deal continues, was very heartening to people who had rather have cows, lizards, and peace than crowds of human consumers of manufacturers' goods.

On Saturday morning, April 22, the program proper of the Texas Folk-Lore Society was inaugurated in the auditorium of the Houston Public Library. President Tsanoff began with a "Preface." The following papers were then read—or talked: "Pie Suppers in East Texas," by Virginia Walker, Overton; "Sheep and Sheepmen in Texas Folk-Lore," by Mrs. Winnifred Kupper, San Antonio; "Baron de Bastrop, God-

178

father of Texas," by Clarence R. Wharton, Houston; "Home Remedies in the Piney Woods of East Texas," by R. G. Upton, Nacogdoches. The attendance was excellent; the contributions were delightful.

After a luncheon at Cohen House on the campus of the Rice Institute, the program was resumed in the lounge room of Cohen House, with addresses as follows: "Legendary Lore of the First Spanish Horses," by Robert Denhart, A. & M. College of Texas, College Station; "Elizabethan Physiognomy and Chiromancy," by Carroll Camden, the Rice Institute, Houston; "Some Bible Folk-Lore," Rabbi Henry Cohen, Galveston; "Where I Have Met the Little Animals," by Dan Storm, Austin. Ray Wood, who gives his address as Raywood, Texas, talked about "Native American Mother Goose Rhymes" in his booklet by that title, and sang some of them.

At five o'clock the Society turned out strong for a complimentary tea given by Miss Ima Hogg at her home in River Oaks.

The program was concluded at night in the auditorium of the Houston Public Library, the room being packed. Contributions were as follows: "Recording Folk-Songs and Fiddle Music" (with phonographic reproductions), by William A. Owens, A. and M. College of Texas, College Station; "The Social Ecology of the American Humorous Anecdote," by Charles Flinn Arrowood, University of Texas, Austin; the Singing of Folk-Songs by a choir of Southwestern University, Georgetown, directed by Henry Meyer; "Folk-Lore and Two Kinds of Culture," by J. Frank Dobie, Austin. The concert of cow horn blowers that was to have been given by Harold F. Graves, Sid Moller, L. J. McNeill, Sr., and L. J. McNeill, Jr., of Brazoria County did not materialize on account of the inability of the leader of the horn men to be present.

The business session of the Society was held in the afternoon. After reports of the treasurer and secretary were

179

received, officers were elected as follows: President, William A. Philpott, Jr., Dallas. Vice-presidents: Charles F. Arrowood, University of Texas, Austin; C. L. Sonnichsen, School of Mines, El Paso; Colonel M. L. Crimmins, Fort Sam Houston, San Antonio. Councillors: Mrs. W. S. Randall, Dallas; Miss Ima Hogg, Houston; Miss Rebecca Smith, Texas Christian University, Fort Worth. Secretary and Editor, J. Frank Dobie, and Associate Editors, Mody C. Boatright and Harry H. Ransom, all three of the University of Texas, Austin. Treasurer, Mrs. Marcelle Lively Hamer, University of Texas, Austin.

INDEX

181

183

INDEX

185

INDEX